FITZROY C. FLETCHER

Fitzroy C. Fletcher

of

Letham Grange

&

Ardmulchan

by

Kathleen G. MacLeman

Typeset in Times Roman 12 point.

A Catalogue Record for this book is available from
The British Library.

Published by
Kathleen Grace MacLeman, Gallowhill, Avoch,
Ross-shire IV9 8QS, Scotland.

Copyright © of the articles in this book rests with the author.
First published in 2000.

No part of this publication may be reproduced, stored in a retrieval system, or transmitted in any form or by any means, electronic, electrostatic, magnetic tape, mechanical, photocopying, recording or otherwise, without permission in writing from the publisher.

ISBN

Designed by ---- Kathleen MacLeman
Typeset by ------ Kathleen MacLeman
Printed by ------ Gospel Truth Press, Castle Road,
 Invergordon, Ross-shire, Scotland.

Kathleen MacLeman 2000.

CONTENTS.

	Page
Preface	i
Introduction	iii
Family Tree	iv
1 - The Pioneer Families	1
2 - Frederica Mary Stephen	15
3 - The History of Letham Grange	27
4 - Ross, Robertson and Rhind	31
5 - The Mansion of Letham Grange	49
6 - Fitzroy Charles Fletcher	85
7 - Letham Grange Estate	103
8 - County Meath, The Boyne and Ardmulchan	113
9 - Arthur George Sydney Mitchell	125
10 - Ardmulchan Castle	143
11 - Frances Mary Grant, Conway and Thomas	165
12 - Postscript	183
13 - Appendix	185
14 - Acknowledgements	187
15 - Illustrations	189
16 - Bibliography	197
17 - Index	201

PREFACE

My memories of Letham Grange as a family home are few and rather shadowy as I was five when my grandfather Conway Fletcher died, but I do recall having tea with my grandmother in the conservatory and lunch in the vast dining-room where a large silver-mounted ram's head glared down threateningly from the sideboard. A market garden selling tomatoes operated from the greenhouses next to the kitchen garden and I can well remember the rows of tomatoes, red and yellow, that stretched for what seemed miles under the glass.

After my grandfather's death, the contents of the house were sold and the building left empty for many years except for a few summers when, for a brief period, it came to life as a hostel for students fruit-picking on the nearby farms. Later still, my sister and I, in our mildly wild youth, would take our friends there in the middle of the night to play "sardines" - great fun in the pitch dark, if not a little ghostly and frightening.

The house was saved from the fate that befell many of its peers - destruction, by a conversion to a hotel and is now a popular location for wedding receptions. I sometimes think that James Fletcher, whose portrait looks down from the staircase, may not have envisaged quite such a future for his mansion, but I am sure that he would approve of its enjoyment by many.

Some years ago I was delighted to read the first book written by Kath MacLeman and three co-authors on Rosehaugh and have been equally delighted to read this second book on Letham Grange and Ardmulchan and to learn, from the massive amount of research she has done, so much more about the history of the houses. I hope you have equal enjoyment in reading this book.

Rosalind Fletcher
September 2000.

Fitzroy Charles Fletcher.
Courtesy of Private Collection.

INTRODUCTION

The famous architect Le Corbusier once said, *"A house is a machine for living in."* Houses, particularly old ones, hold a fascination for many but the lives of the owners and the people who lived in them are no less fascinating.

The history of the Stephen, Hamilton and Grant families whose Scottish origins lay in Aberdeenshire, Ayrshire and Kingussie, may initially seem remote from the life of Fitzroy Charles Fletcher but through a series of marriages they all became intertwined and part of the Fletcher family. Fitzroy's father was born as James Jack in Elgin but changed his surname in later life to his mother's maiden name of Fletcher. For detailed information on the Jack/Fletcher origins and of James Douglas Fletcher, brother of Fitzroy, the reader should refer to the book "Rosehaugh - A House of its Time."

Fitzroy Charles Fletcher inherited the mansion of Letham Grange in Angus along with considerable wealth but he used this resource as a creative power for the benefit of others as well as himself. It was through this affluence that the Inverness architects, John Rhind and John Robertson were commissioned by Fitzroy's father to alter Letham Grange House and also by which means the gifted ability of Edinburgh architect, Sydney Mitchell was utilised by Fitzroy for the construction of Ardmulchan House in County Meath in Ireland.

This is a story of two mansions but it is also a story of the lives of people who lived in a bygone era. It is hoped that the use of photographs will aid the enjoyment of the varied chapters.

STEPHEN

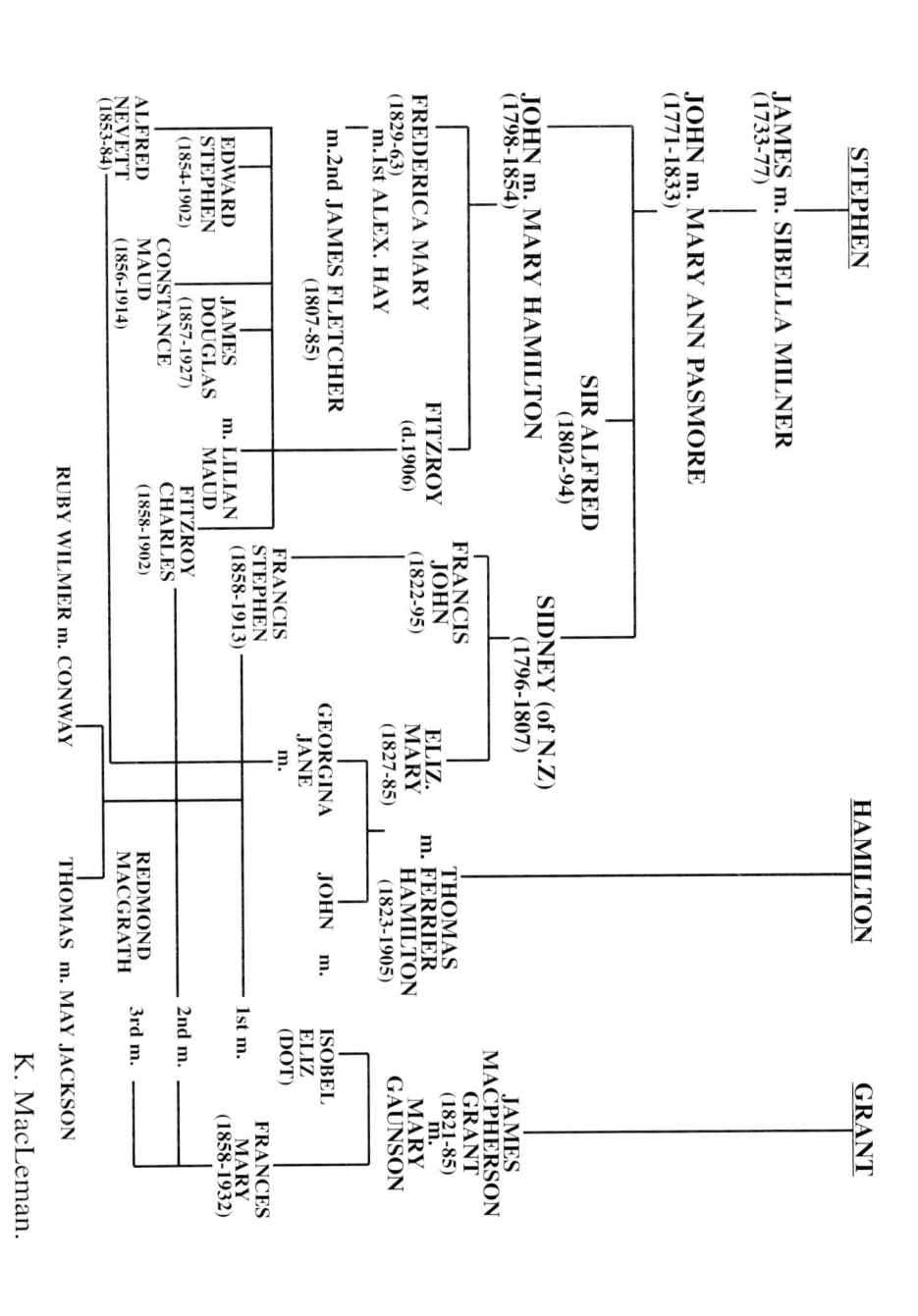

JAMES m. SIBELLA MILNER
(1733-77)
│
├── JOHN m. MARY ANN PASMORE
│   (1771-1833)
│   │
│   ├── JOHN m. MARY HAMILTON
│   │   (1798-1854)
│   │   │
│   │   ├── FREDERICA MARY ── FITZROY
│   │   │   (1829-63)   (d.1906)
│   │   │   m.1st ALEX. HAY
│   │   │   m.2nd JAMES FLETCHER
│   │   │   (1807-85)
│   │   │   │
│   │   │   ├── EDWARD STEPHEN
│   │   │   │   (1854-1902)
│   │   │   ├── JAMES DOUGLAS ── m. LILIAN MAUD
│   │   │   │   (1857-1927)
│   │   │   ├── ALFRED NEVETT
│   │   │   │   (1853-84)
│   │   │   ├── CONSTANCE MAUD
│   │   │   │   (1856-1914)
│   │   │   └── FITZROY CHARLES
│   │   │   (1858-1902)
│   │   │
│   │   └── SIR ALFRED
│   │   (1802-94)
│   │
│   └── SIDNEY (of N.Z)
│   (1796-1807)
│   │
│   ├── FRANCIS JOHN
│   │   (1822-95)
│   │   │
│   │   └── FRANCIS STEPHEN
│   │   (1858-1913)
│   │   m. GEORGINA JANE
│   │   │
│   │   1st m. ── JOHN
│   │   2nd m. ── REDMOND MACGRATH
│   │   3rd m. ──
│   │
│   └── ELIZ. MARY ── m. THOMAS FERRIER HAMILTON
│   (1827-85)   (1823-1905) **HAMILTON**

RUBY WILMER m. CONWAY

THOMAS m. MAY JACKSON

K. MacLeman.

GRANT

JAMES MACPHERSON GRANT ── m. MARY GAUNSON
(1821-85)
│
├── ISOBEL ELIZ (DOT)
└── FRANCES MARY
    (1858-1932)

THE PIONEER FAMILIES

The early history of Australia has been well documented but it is easy to forget that its development was a recent one in comparison with that of Europe. When an independent America decided to cease the depositing by the British Government of sickly and aged convicts on its shores, a speedy alternative had to be found and in the 1780s laden "convict" ships were directed to Australia, landing their human cargo at Sydney.

By the early 1800s life in Britain had become intolerable for many: soldiers returning from the Napoleonic Wars were faced with unemployment and their families with severe hardship; in the Scottish Highlands absentee lairds, living beyond their means in extravagant style in the cities, bled the life blood from their estates by imposing extortionate rents which left tenants there at starvation level. Large numbers moved from the beleaguered inland estates to the coast. Between 1791 and 1821 there was such a rapid growth of population in the Hebrides and the Isle of Skye that the land reached an unsustainable level. Starvation was again commonplace.

The rural areas of Britain were not without knowledge of world events. The development of road systems and the innovation of local newspapers carried the word, despite many being illiterate. A quote, which on this occasion is attributed to the Inverness Courier, is very appropriate:

" The Courier took the news of the Empire to the people and the people took off to the Empire."

With the plight of many in Britain now desperate, the British Government began encouraging emigration and provided cheap or free passage to the new lands. Between the years of 1820 and 1914 an astounding 16,000,000 people emigrated.

In 1824 the greater part of Australia was still unexplored. Earlier attempts at colonisation had met with failure, the only settlements being at Sydney where the people were totally dependent on incoming ships for supplies. Lack of water was a major problem. As explorers progressed gradually south of Sydney, glowing reports filtered back to Britain of the area now known as Victoria. This was pioneer country.

1a   AUSTRALIA - pre 1828

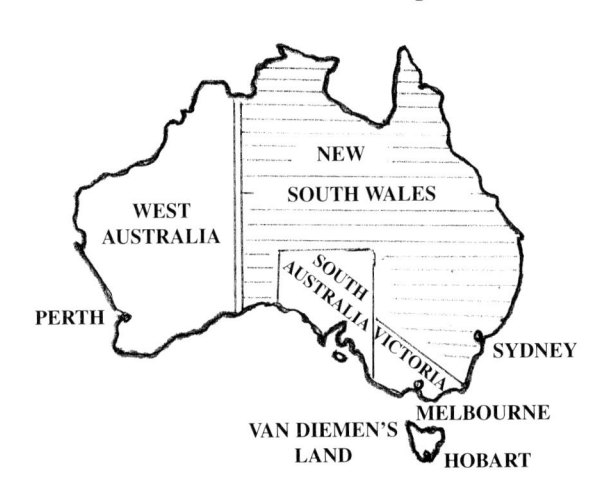

1b   AUSTRALIA - circa 1855

Of the families which went forth, the fortunes of the Stephen, Hamilton and Grant families are of particular interest in relation to the Fletchers.

THE STEPHEN FAMILY

The origins of the Stephen family lie in Aberdeenshire but later generations moved south and the children of James Stephen achieved considerable success in the field of medicine and Government and in the legal profession. Of the next generation almost all chose the Law for careers and with due diligence, one became Colonial Under-Secretary with the title of Right Honourable Sir; another, who was a Queen's Counsel, was knighted and a third was Judge Commissioner of the Court of Bankruptcy at Bristol. The Stephen family was clearly successfully established in the legal profession.

John Stephen, third son of the aforementioned James, ventured to St. Kitts, one of the Leeward Islands, where he was later appointed Solicitor General. Promotion in the legal and diplomatic services of that time often necessitated the acceptance of postings to the remote out-reaches of the Empire, though St. Kitts was the first successful colony of the British West Indies. Several British merchants were already established in the Leeward Islands as owners of sugar plantations and exploiters of the slave trade, a trade which another member of the family, James Fitzjames Stephen, was active in having abolished.

Living conditions in St. Kitts could not have been easy for the wives and Mary Ann Pasmore, John's wife, went to America to have their second son, though a later son, George, died at St. Kitts when aged ten. The older sons were educated at schools in Britain and returned to the Leeward Islands for a period before progressing to legal positions in the developing countries of Australia and New Zealand. Their father, John Stephen, accompanied by his wife and younger children had already preceded them to Australia in 1824, sailing to Sydney on the "Prince Regent" for his new appointment as Solicitor General in New South Wales.

2. The Prince Regent (Capt. Cowper Phipps Coles)
Courtesy of National Maritime Museum, London.

In 1824 New South Wales and Van Diemen's Land, now Tasmania, were regulated by the same legal body and under a monopoly. Months after his arrival, John became an acting judge of the Supreme Court and in the following year his sons Sidney and Alfred were given legal appointments - Alfred to Hobart in Van Diemen's Land and Sidney to the city of Sydney. Their ability was not in question but their appointments may have appeared to some as a patriarchal move particularly as such appointments were instructed from London where their cousin was the Colonial Under-Secretary. He, for his part, not only required a person of ability for the position but one whom he could trust.

In 1839 Sidney also moved to Hobart where he practised successfully as a barrister and advocate until 1842 when he had an unfortunate "collision" with Mr. Justice Montague who had him debarred from practising in any Court in the Colony of Australia. This was quite an act of revenge and a five-year battle ensued to have him reinstated, an appeal proceeding through many channels until brought before the Privy Council of the Home Government. In spite of the Council finding that there was no case to answer, Sidney's career had suffered irreparable damage and he was brought to the brink of bankruptcy. Finally, in 1847, the Privy Council made the following pronouncement :-

" It is very much to be lamented that the Court took the course they did in this case. Without pronouncing any censure upon the Judges for the injurious language which they used, or the mistaken course which they pursued, justice to Mr. Stephen's character compels their Lordships to declare that there is nothing whatever in the whole case casting an imputation upon him, and that he leaves the Court with his private character and his professional conduct altogether unimpeached. "

Historical Records of Australia.

3. "Sidney Stephen" by A.B. Cambridge (1909)
The painting was commissioned after Sidney's death and the original hangs in the Court at Otago, New Zealand.

During these five dark years, Sidney moved to Melbourne with his family where he tried to make a living in agriculture. Even in this venture there was to be conflict with the legal establishment. Sidney was a staunch supporter of the Wesleyan faith, generous to the poor and a clever lawyer, yet his career was littered with personal altercations with representatives of legal authority. He was prone to being involved in lawsuits but more often with himself as the defendant than as the defendant's lawyer. On selling his farm he came under severe censure by the Court for not fulfilling the full agreement of the transaction which entailed selling the human workforce along with the land. Such a transaction was totally against Sidney's principles.

Though the Privy Council had now restored his professional standing, any optimistic plans to return to his profession soon foundered. The Colonial legal monopoly stated that there was no suitable opening for him and three years elapsed before Sidney left the shores of Australia for New Zealand where initially he was assigned a relatively modest position.

With his experience and ability, he soon rose to the position of acting Chief Justice of the Supreme Court in New Zealand and the Colonial establishment were content to leave him in that situation. The earlier years of stress had affected his health and he died in 1857. Of his family, his daughter Elizabeth Mary Milner Stephen and his grandson Francis Sidney Stephen are of interest for their indirect ties to the Fletchers with Francis Sidney's sons later assuming the name of Fletcher.

The most prominent of the Stephens in Australia was Sidney's brother Alfred who played an important part in the evolution of Australia's legal and political systems. Also born at St Christopher, St. Kitts and educated in England, he returned to the West Indies for some years before studying law in London. After being called to the Bar in 1823, he sailed for Hobart, Van Diemen's Land in 1825 and within months was appointed Solicitor General. When still only 27, Alfred discovered an important error in Australian land titles. The error was rectified and he was rewarded with the position of Attorney General of Van Diemen's Land, a post in which he worked diligently for four years. His future in the Australian legal profession was secured.

His ambitions, however, lay higher, and after a short spell in private practice he moved to Sydney where he secured the position of acting Judge of the Supreme Court. In the years which ensued, Alfred progressed steadily up the legal ladder, not only executing his judicial duties but now also advising the Government on complicated legislative questions. He was totally committed to his profession and apart from a year's leave of absence spent in Europe, he served continuously on the Legislative Council from 1856 till his retirement in 1891 at the age of 89 years. In the course of this lengthy period he was largely instrumental in drafting the Criminal Law Amendment Bill and towards his retirement he became interested in amending the law of divorce.

4. Sir Alfred Stephen - Photograph by Newman.
Australian Portrait Gallery of Representative Colonial Men.

During this long life he married twice, had 18 children and when he died at the age of 92 there were 66 grandchildren. As a judge he was considered severe but he believed in carrying out the Law as it was written. Universally respected, he had, without doubt, made a great contribution to the legal system of a developing country, a fact reflected on the honours bestowed on him :-

Sir Alfred Stephen, CB; KCMG; GCMG; PC.

Such honours were frequently embellished by the addition of a coat of Arms and Alfred had his registered in Britain as well as in Australia with the motto "Virtus Ubique" meaning "Moral excellence everywhere."

5. ARMS OF SIR ALFRED STEPHEN

The double-headed eagle with displayed wings signifies one involved in important affairs and of sound judgement in matters of equivocatory meaning. The outstretched wings denote protection to those who require it and the gripping talons threaten ruin and punishment to all that break the Law. The open hand is a pledge of justice and sincerity. The chevron, crescent and mullet or star all suggest one who has given faithful service, who has benefited from learning and religion and to whom is attributed the qualities of virtue and piety.

Sir Alfred and Sidney Stephen were the uncles of Frederica Mary Stephen who is the connecting link with the Fletchers. Frederica's father John was born in America in 1798 and coincidentally his wife-to-be, Mary Matthew Hamilton, daughter of a British Army Colonel, was also born in America at Virginia. They were married in London in 1821 and with their first three children decided to join his parents in the new lands of Australia, sailing for Sydney aboard the "Admiral Cockburn" in 1827. At Sydney, John held the posts of Land Commissioner and J.P. but they returned to Britain in 1829 with a petition and Frederica, their only daughter, was born in that year at Jersey. In 1833 they again faced the arduous voyage to Sydney in the "Westmoreland".

It seems quite admirable that people with young families would face such long and often dangerous journeys. The medical profession of the time, when confronted with no other means of a cure for wealthy patients, would frequently recommend a voyage to Australia. The unfortunate demise of any such patients would then surely be associated with the hazards of the voyage rather than with a failure to cure. One such trip from Germany to Melbourne in the middle to late 1800s was considered a "fast sailing" when completed in 81 days. The record for a sailing ship covering the journey from Britain to Sydney, even with favourable winds, still took over 68 days. Disembarking at Melbourne could reduce the length of the voyage by as much as a week but in the early 1800s there was little incentive to do so as it consisted then purely of "outback".

It was not until 1835 that Melbourne was founded, and then only as a small village settlement. John Stephen, however, felt that there was potential in this frontier village and moved his family there in 1839. His instincts were correct but unfortunately he did not survive long enough to reap the benefits, dying at St. Kilda, Melbourne in 1854 aged 66. His widow Mary Matthew Hamilton, his daughter Frederica and his son Fitzroy were all closely linked with James Fletcher.

THE HAMILTON FAMILY

In Scotland the family inheritance was usually the birthright of the eldest son, a right which left other sons seeking their fortunes in military careers or in adventures in the Colonies. In the same year that John Stephen moved to Melbourne, yet another young Scot seeking his fortune arrived at Sydney on the " Abberton ". Aged only 19, Thomas Ferrier Hamilton, the 3rd. Son of Colonel John Ferrier Hamilton of Cairnhill and Westport in Scotland had sailed to Australia with his cousin.

The first permanent settlers to Melbourne had crossed the Bass Strait from Tasmania but the spreading reports of this green and pleasant land caused others like Thomas Hamilton to venture to the Melbourne area. Thomas and his cousin rode from Sydney to Port Phillip on the south coast and there they took title of land in the Gisbourne area to the north-west of Melbourne, hilly land at the foot of the Australian Alps. The two young men named the area of land Cairnhill and formed a partnership in 1839. This partnership was dissolved in 1861 and Thomas moved to New Gisbourne, acquiring a property called Eldersie where he built a home for his ever-extending family. He had married well: his wife was Elizabeth Mary Milner Stephen, a daughter of Chief Justice Sidney Stephen of New Zealand. They had eleven children. Thomas involved himself in local affairs, being J.P. and magistrate, and was an ardent player of cricket though his ability as bowler was much superior to that of batsman.

Victoria became an independent state in 1851 and so Thomas's position of magistrate and later as a member of Victoria's Legislative Council was of importance. His political interests lay in an extension of the railway system, free education and in the improvement of legislation.

Of his eleven children, John Ferrier Hamilton the eldest son, and Georgina Jane Vereker Hamilton the eldest daughter have connections through the sons of James Fletcher.

THE GRANT FAMILY

Of the three families it could be said that James MacPherson Grant achieved the most. The Stephen and Hamilton families had set out for Australia with the advantages of superior education, parental position and contacts. James, on the other hand, set out with only a basic education and an undiluted Highland determination to succeed.

He was born in 1821 to Lewis Grant, a plumber, and Isobel MacBain of Braeruthven, in a small hill croft above Ruthven Barracks, Kingussie. The family moved later to the Balavil Estate, two miles away. James received his early education at Kingussie, which offered an exceptional standard of education for such a small community. Provision for a basic but narrow education had been in existence from the early 1700s, particularly during the winter months when the children were not working on the crofts. Kingussie School was the starting point of careers for many young men.

There was much poverty in the district and much talk of emigration. Though a somewhat isolated community, Kingussie benefited from a position on the Great North Road with all travel and news from Edinburgh and the south passing its threshold on the way north. In 1836 James, his parents, brothers and sisters sailed to Sydney.

Having no obvious avenues open to him, his first venture, while still a teenager, took him to New Zealand as a volunteer in the Army fighting the Maoris. This was not to his taste and he returned to Sydney where he entered the legal profession being articled to the firm of Chambers and Thurlow during the years 1841 to 1847. On the successful completion of his training and now as Mr. Thurlow's partner, James decided to charter a trading vessel to voyage to California. The reason for such a move is not clear but the timing coincided with the Californian Gold Rush of 1848. This venture also profited him nothing.

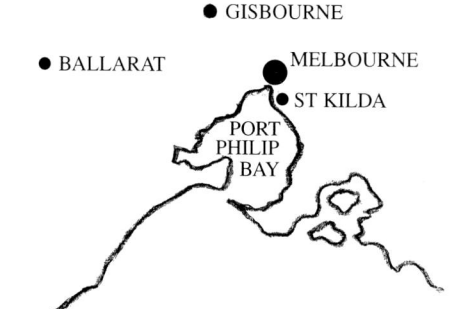

6. The Melbourne Area of Australia - circa 1855

    Though Melbourne and the surrounding area had seen a small but steady growth of settlers during the years between 1835 and 1850, it was still part of the State of New South Wales. In 1851 an Australian who had gained experience in the gold fields of California returned home and discovered gold at Bendigo. Further finds at Ballarat, Castlemaine and Bunnyong created a massive explosion of population at Melbourne. The politically maturing Legislative Council of Melbourne seized this opportunity and succeeded in having the necessary legislation passed at Sydney. The State of Victoria came into being, separate from New South Wales.

    Never one to miss an opportunity, James headed for the gold fields of Bendigo and though disappointment was yet again to be his only reward, the first hand experience gained there was to be of great value to him a few years later. Disillusioned, he returned to continue his legal duties.

    The incident at the Eureka Stockade in 1854 is well documented and even referred to by some academics as being "the catalyst for true Australian democracy." The miners in the gold fields had many longstanding grievances against the establishment- no vote, police corruption, and extortionate charges for the right to mine. This situation was fuelled further by the acquittal of an hotel owner, Bentley, who had kicked a miner to death. Enraged miners rioted and burnt down Bentley's hotel, an action for which three of them were arrested. The other miners organised themselves into the Ballarat Reform League and demanded the right of adults to choose their own members of Parliament as well as the abolition of miners' licences. When they erected a stockade across the streets of Ballarat and raised what they referred to as the " new Australian flag ", rumour circulated of plans to create a republic. The authorities took panic and ordered the Government troops to attack. In less than thirty minutes, 22 men and 6 soldiers lay dead. Thirty miners were charged with high treason.

Without any question of a fee, James MacPherson Grant took on the defence of the miners, making much use of his own experience and knowledge of their grievances. They were all acquitted and as a result of their stand, the British Government in 1855 allowed Australia to elect its own Houses of Parliament and the Colony was set on the path to self-government.

James, now married, settled in Melbourne and was elected to the Legislative Assembly of Victoria in which he held numerous ministerial positions. One particularly important piece of legislation which he succeeded in having passed was the Land Act of 1869, an Act which formed the basis of all subsequent land settlements in Victoria. He did much in the way of settling the people on public lands.

James retired from public life as Chief Secretary of the Legislative Council of Victoria and died two years later at the age of 64. The Scottish connection was rekindled after his death when his daughter, Frances Mary, who first married Francis Sidney Stephen, grandson of Sidney Stephen, Chief Justice of the Supreme Court of New Zealand, later married Fitzroy Charles Fletcher of Letham Grange in Scotland. James's widow and two daughters all died at Letham Grange and were buried at St. Vigeans churchyard.

FREDERICA MARY STEPHEN

Frederica Mary Stephen was born in 1829 during the return visit made by her parents to Britain from Australia and was the first connecting link between the Stephen and Fletcher families. Blonde, reserved and the only daughter of John and Mary Stephen, she was barely four when the family made the long journey back to Australia and only ten when they moved from Sydney to the small settlement of Melbourne.

7. Frederica Mary Stephen.
Courtesy of John Shaw of Tordarroch.

It was customary for daughters to be married at the earliest opportunity and much social advancement could be gained by appropriate marriages into monied or titled families. Frederica was married in Australia at the age of sixteen to Alexander MacLeod Hay of Westerton, Scotland, a Lieutenant in the 58th Regiment of Foot and on duty in the Colonies. Their marriage took place at Port Macquarie, New South Wales but soon afterwards Alexander was posted to Auckland, New Zealand where the Maori people were in revolt. It was at Auckland, three years after the marriage, that he was tragically killed at 30 years of age in September 1848, just months before the birth of his daughter Mary MacLeod Hay.

Alexander was the eldest son of Colonel Alexander Hay who had spent 20 years in India where he had acquired considerable wealth. On returning to Scotland, Colonel Hay purchased the Westerton Estate close to Pluscarden, Elgin in 1813. His wealth was used to carry out much needed improvements on the neglected Estate - draining large areas, planting, and breaking in expanses of moorland. His efforts were then enhanced with the building of a handsome, two storey, castellated mansion of red and grey granite quarried on the estate. The lintels, cornices and ornamental mouldings were of a smoothly dressed freestone and a large Gothic window soared above the principal entrance giving light to the main hall inside. The building, surrounded by carefully planned lawns, garden beds and fish pond, overlooked a picturesque artificial lake which extended to over two acres and was separated from the lawn by laurel and bay trees.

Being the oldest son, Alexander would have been expected to return and inherit Westerton after his term of duty in the Army, but the father died the same year of Alexander's marriage to Frederica in Australia. With Alexander's death following soon after, the Estate fell to the second son, David, who also died within a few years. Several changes of ownership caused the fortunes of the estate to gradually diminish. In the 20th century it was purchased by the Wills Family of the tobacco industry. The mansion had been

8. WESTERTOWN - Seat of Colonel Alexander Hay

Etching by W. Read

much neglected during the frequent changes of ownership and was requiring a great amount of renovation; but fate intervened and it was totally consumed by fire. A modern house of lesser proportions now stands on the site.

Frederica, who, in the space of little more than four years, had been bride, wife, mother and now widow, returned to live with her parents at Melbourne.

There is nothing to suggest where James Jack, later Fletcher, met Frederica. Considering the entrepreneurial character of the man, it is very possible that the discovery of gold in Victoria in 1851 coupled with the potential for the development of communications in the Colony would have attracted his interest.

In a twenty-year period, James, alongside his brother, had amassed great wealth as a merchant based in Liverpool and trading from Peru. Though still involved in the business of trading, shrewd and large investments in railways and mines worldwide had served to increase his fortune. His insatiable appetite for financial growth would have meant that the developing situation at Melbourne would have been irresistible to him. John Stephen, Frederica's father, was a local dignitary and it is likely that he would have entertained James at his home. James was unmarried, wealthy and surely a very desirable husband for a young widow.

The marriage of Frederica, aged 23 and James, now 45, took place at St George's Church, Hanover Square, London on the 21st July 1852 and the first child, a son, was born in May 1853.

After his long residence in Peru, James had purchased Woolton Hill House in the suburbs of Liverpool in 1850, doubtless with a view to marriage and family. Though this house now became home to Frederica, many excursions were still made abroad. It was customary for those with wealth to sojourn in the south of France during late spring or early summer and it must have been on such a visit that Frederica met a grand-uncle, William Pasmore, who wrote her a letter from France after her return to Liverpool. Dated June 1854, it is addressed to Mrs Jack, as it was not until the following year that the surname Jack was changed to Fletcher.

The Fitzroy mentioned in the letter was Frederica's brother.

9. The cover and words of the letter sent by W.T.Pasmore.
Courtesy of M. MacLeman.

"I would go to Australia to see my relatives on my Father's side & my early friends; for as to the time of life, the comfort & ease of the large steamers are such that a person of eighty might well attempt the voyage. My sister Sibylla regretted more than you did that she did not arrive in time to see you & take you by the hand, for in speaking of you, you had a good advocate & every word I said augmented her wish to have seen her relative and made a friend. I am waiting still for fine weather to start on my summer excursion, for we still have 3 days rain for one day of sun. I have

been very ill since your departure as one night, in a severe fit of coughing I broke a blood vessel & the blood gushed from my mouth in a fearful manner. The loss of my vital liquid made me very weak & irritated my nervous system to such a point that I was in a state of shuddering all day. It also brought on low fever & sent me back to quinine. I am now getting well again but am very thin & weak & of a yellow hue. Pray give my best regards to Mr. Jack; my sincere & affectionate friendship to Fitzroy & of course to Miss Brown, my most gallant souvenir. To you my dear Frederica I send the strongest wishes for your happiness & my sincere esteem & true affection.
W.T.Pasmore"
Courtesy of M. MacLeman.

On her return from France, Frederica was four months into her second pregnancy and a second son was born in November followed by a daughter in 1856 and two more sons in June 1857 and November 1858. She was not of a strong constitution and these consecutive pregnancies affected her health. A congestion of the lungs developed into tuberculosis. It is perhaps significant that Frederica was resident at Woolton Hill House in April of 1861 when the census was held. The gentry were normally abroad at that time of year, in the Colonies or in the south of France. She did however have the company of her daughter Mary Hay, now 12 years, and she also received a visit from Lieutenant Colonel Charles Thompson and his wife, of the 58th Regiment of Foot, her first husband's regiment.

It was perhaps a last futile hope for medical treatment which took James and Frederica, now in a frail and critical condition, to Edinburgh. Liver congestion and kidney failure signified her final days and she died at 19 Abercromby Place, Edinburgh in September 1863, at only 34 years of age. Her youngest child Fitzroy Charles was barely five.

James, still heavily involved with business interests, was now sole parent of five young children but Mary Matthew Stephen,

Frederica's mother and widow since 1854, visited from Australia and shared in her grandchildren's upbringing.

The fortunes of Frederica's children varied considerably and doubtless the death of their mother when they were so young would have affected them. The children had been primarily educated privately at home at Woolton Hill House, Liverpool and then, as each son attained fourteen, they were sent to Eton. For James Douglas and the youngest, Fitzroy Charles, both sensitive, almost shy like their mother, the Eton experience must have been a difficult one but they made friendships there which endured the years, as recorded in the visitors' album for Rosehaugh during 1900 to 1904. Many friends had distinguished themselves in military exploits or in the field of commerce and the names of Vandeleur, Wyndham, Tweeddale, Cunard and Stanley are only but a few of those recorded.

James Fletcher, the father, had purchased Rosehaugh Estate in 1865 and the pure, bracing Highland air coupled with the freedom which the grounds allowed must have been a great source of enjoyment to the children when on holiday there.

The eldest, Alfred Nevett, had a strong adventurous spirit, which resisted all efforts by his father to channel it constructively. Having mingled in unacceptable company for some time, he was sent to his Australian relatives and returned in 1881 with a wife, Georgina Jane Vereker Hamilton, eldest daughter of Thomas Ferrier Hamilton of Melbourne. Alfred's earlier lifestyle, however, took its toll and he died at the untimely age of thirty-one leaving no children.

Edward Stephen, the second son, had not been expected to survive at birth and his delicate condition and mental limitations meant a lifetime of care.

The only daughter, Constance Maud, inherited her father's colouring as well as his strength of will. Her marriage to Captain Montagu Hope of Luffness at Inverness in November 1876 was a great local occasion and a marvellous opportunity for James, her father, to demonstrate to all his wealth and organising ability. (For

10. Constance Maud Fletcher.
Painted by Colin Hunter at Rosehaugh in 1873.
Courtesy of John Shaw of Tordarroch.

11. James Fletcher (The father).
Drawing by Colin Hunter at Rosehaugh in August 1878.
Courtesy of Private Collection.

a detailed report on the local celebrations and a list of those who attended - see Appendix) Regrettably, despite the birth of a daughter, the marriage did not survive many years. Customs of that era made Constance's situation socially unacceptable and she went to America during the proceedings of divorce in 1882. There is no record of her having returned to Britain but it is known that she died in 1914.

The life of James Douglas Fletcher has been covered in detail in the book "Rosehaugh" and it is sufficient to say that he spent a comfortable life as laird of his estates in the North of Scotland. His grandmother, Mary Matthew Stephen, had remained in contact and was resident at Rosehaugh when she died in1891, aged 87 years. Her son Fitzroy Stephen, Colonel of the Rifle Brigade, and his wife Frances were also living at Rosehaugh at this time with some of their children. James Douglas later married their fourth daughter, Lilian Maud Augusta.

Fitzroy Fletcher's stay at Eton was relatively short, leaving after two and a half years but, at the age of eighteen, he embarked on a lengthy educational tour of Europe, studying at both Weimar in Saxony and at Paris. This accounted for his absence at the splendid affair of his sister's wedding in November 1876.

On his return from the Continent two years later, Fitzroy enlisted in the 2nd Dragoons of the Royal Scots Greys, a heavy cavalry regiment, which had distinguished itself many times on the battlefield, particularly at Waterloo and Balaclava. It was the oldest regiment of Dragoons in the British Army and raised in Scotland in the mid seventeenth century with the motto "Second to None". James Fletcher must have been proud of his son's commission. With bearskin and white plume, a blazing red tunic over blue trousers, all accompanied with a sword, Fitzroy was a striking figure in uniform. It was during his time with the Regiment that Fitzroy discovered his great affinity with horses, an attachment which he was able to indulge when he became owner of Letham Grange.

12. Fitzroy Charles Fletcher in the uniform
of the Royal Scots Greys.
Courtesy of Private Collection.

James Fletcher was now of advancing years and with concern for the continuance of his "Empire", he recalled James Douglas and Fitzroy to Rosehaugh in 1883 to prime them on the management of their future inheritance. James died in 1885 and whilst James Douglas inherited Rosehaugh and Woolton Hill House in Liverpool, Fitzroy was now proprietor of Letham Grange and Fern Estates in Angus and Forfar. Throughout his life James had been perceptive and astute in business transactions, leaving nothing to chance. These characteristics permeated his Will. Fitzroy's instructions were to complete the renovations and improvements begun by his father at Letham Grange. In order to achieve this, the Executors were permitted to make an allowance of not more that £15,000 and not less that £5,000 for the completion and furnishing of the House and outbuildings and the planting of the gardens and grounds.

HISTORY OF LETHAM GRANGE

James Fletcher of Rosehaugh, in his purchase of Letham Grange Estate in 1877 from the Trustees of the Hay family for the sum of £121,800, also acquired an important part of Forfarshire history covering more than three centuries.

The earliest mention of the lands of Letham is recorded in the annals of Arbroath History for 1284 when Abbot William gave the life-rent of these lands to one called Hugo Heem. Further references do not occur until the late 15th and early 16th centuries when the Dedication of St. Vigeans Church with two great altars took place at the instance of a local devout man, John Brown, tenant of Letham. John Brown may have been a somewhat paradoxical character, devout, wealthy and donor of the rents of property to the Church for the salvation of his soul ----- and those of his three wives. His instructions regarding the order of the annual service for their souls were explicit. The service had to be conducted by six priests and three boys with an additional clause stating - *"if the chaplain be caught keeping a concubine or firelighter for the space of one month or forty days, then my successors will cease the granting of this endowment."*

There is an interesting historical connection between the name of St. Vigeans and Ireland, the dedication name being derived from the 7th century Irish saint, St. Fechin, who was Abbot of Fohbar or Fore in Westmeath, a district not far distant from the Ardmulchan Estate which Fitzroy Fletcher later purchased. It would seem that St. Fechin sent forth his followers on a mission to bring Christianity to the Angus area. He himself died in a widespread famine in 665 but his followers established a form of church in the area of St Vigeans, which survived from these early times. The name of St. Vigeans preserves historical reminiscences of a time when a close fellowship existed between the Churches of Scotland and Ireland, a fellowship which did not exist with the English Churches of that era. The numerous Celtic crosses at St. Vigeans are very similar to those of the Irish Celtic period.

In 1526 the Wood family of Bonnington from the district of Montrose took lease of Letham from the Abbey. They later became owners but resided in town during the winter months. Letham remained in the Wood family for many years but in the time of Sir James Wood, an eminent soldier during the reign of Queen Anne serving under the Duke of Marlborough as Colonel of the Scots Fusiliers, most of the family lands were sold and Letham was purchased by a Robert Stephen whose sundial inscribed "R.S. 1773" stood in the gardens of the old house until removed by Fitzroy Fletcher to the front of the present mansion.

There was a further change of ownership in 1803 when it was acquired by Alexander Hay, a merchant and manufacturer in Arbroath. Already a proprietor of several buildings in the town, Mr. Hay soon added the neighbouring estate of Peebles to that of Letham and in 1822 he extended his lands still further with the purchase of New Grange Estate. It was the first time that one family owned all three estates and the Hays were first to give the combined lands the name of Letham Grange, which was then the most extensive estate in the parish of St. Vigeans.

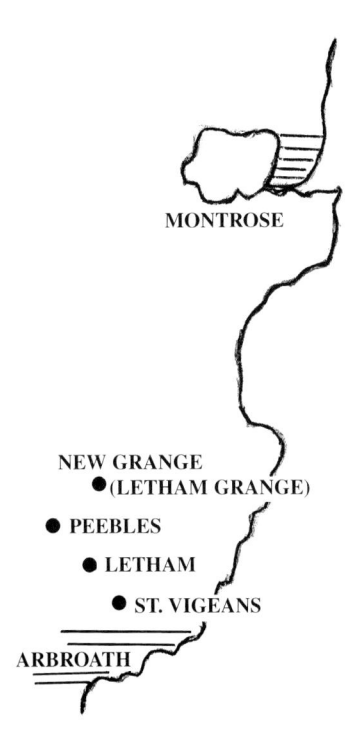

13. Map showing the sites of Letham, Peebles and New Grange Estates.

Such an expanse of land necessitated the building of a mansion of appropriate proportions and John Hay, having become the Laird after his father, commissioned the Aberdeen architect Archibald Simpson to build him such a mansion in 1827. The position chosen was on a natural terrace overlooking the valley of the river Brothock and virtually on the site of the old house of New Grange which Archibald Simpson transformed from a mundane farmhouse to a spacious dwelling with a portico facing a south-west exposure.

14. Letham Grange - 1827 by Archibald Simpson, architect.

John Hay was a typical country gentleman known locally as "Squire" Hay, a title rarely used in Scotland. He was knowledgeable with a "good taste in literature", hospitable and a good landowner. As an enthusiastic sportsman, he had his own pack of hounds at Letham Grange but he had an equally enthusiastic dislike of poachers. He remained a bachelor and when he died in 1869 his estate was left in trust for his grandnephew John Hay Miln. Unfortunately the estate was encumbered to three-quarters of its value and the trustees sold it to James Fletcher of Rosehaugh in February 1877.

15. Part of the entrance arch and gates of Letham Grange.

ROSS, ROBERTSON AND RHIND

All three architects were fortunate to be living and working in the Highlands during a period of great change which saw the development of an educational system and a new mode of travel by rail which created the development of country estates for the sporting pursuits of the gentry. These produced benefits for architects and the construction industry.

In 1860, travel to and from Inverness was by mail coach or water conveyance only. The mail coach to Dunkeld left daily at five-thirty in the morning and arrived at Dunkeld at five o'clock in the evening in time to catch the train to Edinburgh, Glasgow or London. The alternative was to board the schooner "Sovereign" which sailed for Aberdeen every Monday evening, calling at Chanonry Point and Cromarty. In order to reach Edinburgh by sea, one caught the "Dundalk" or "Kangaroo" every Thursday afternoon from Inverness calling at all ports. Glasgow could only be reached by water during the months of July, August and September via the Caledonian Canal.

The arrival of the railway at Inverness had far-reaching consequences for the Highlands by making the region accessible to those with wealth in the south. A shooting and fishing estate in the Highlands was a status symbol for anyone of importance and many large country houses, shooting lodges and stables were constructed. The railway also brought gentry escaping the summer heat of the cities and new hotels were built to meet the increased demand for accommodation. As visitor numbers increased, so did the wealth of local tradesmen and merchants who in turn built new and larger homes in keeping with their newly-acquired wealth.

A massive building programme resulted from the Scottish Education Act of 1875 with schools and schoolhouses requiring to be erected all over the north. The ecclesiastical fraternity were not to be bereft of attention during this explosion of development.

The Disruption of the Church of Scotland in 1843 and continuing schisms within the Church all created a need for many new church buildings and manses.

For Ross, Robertson and Rhind, the years between 1860 and 1900 were years of golden opportunity but not all three fared equally.

ALEXANDER ROSS

Alexander Ross, architect, benefited greatly from the outset of these economic developments and it is interesting to note that he was born in 1834 at Brechin which is not too distant from Letham Grange. His father, James, assisted the architect Archibald Simpson who designed the original mansion house at Letham Grange. Simpson also drew the plans for Raigmore House for the MacIntosh family at Inverness and James Ross, along with his family, was transferred north to work on it. Having settled in Inverness, James set up his own business but his early death left Alexander, still only nineteen, in charge. In 1860 Alexander was employed by Sir Alexander Matheson of Ardross and through this position he made contacts leading to many prestigious work opportunities.

JOHN ROBERTSON

Of the three architects, John Robertson was the only one native to Inverness, born at Castlehill of Inshes to Margaret Campbell and Alexander Robertson, a carpenter, in November 1840. Unlike Ross and Rhind, both of whom inherited family concerns already established in architecture, John began as an apprentice in the offices of Alexander Ross under whose guidance he developed his talents, becoming a skilful draughtsman and a gifted designer of the classical lines of architecture.

When James Fletcher purchased Rosehaugh Estate in Ross-shire, he introduced major agricultural improvements, reducing the number of small holdings to create larger and economically viable units. During the years 1870 to 1878, James made much use of the services of Alexander Ross particularly in the building of impressive farmhouses on the newly formed units. At least seventeen farmhouses were constructed on the Estate in this period. Ross was also commissioned by James to alter and add to Rosehaugh mansion house, alter the stable block, create new and impressive entrance gates and lodge, and design the Avoch Free Church. Being such a prolific architect, Ross could not have attended to all the work in hand and it was doubtless John Robertson who supervised much of the work at Rosehaugh where he would have made the acquaintance of James Fletcher.

Many prestigious commissions and an astute business mind resulted in a financial security for Alexander Ross that permitted travels in Europe and created the status of an important local personage, particularly so when he later became Provost of Inverness and also received a doctorate from Aberdeen University. Even in 1880 his fees possibly reflected this popularity and as James Fletcher was noted for his appreciation of "value for money", and Robertson was already supervising much of the work for Ross, this would seem to be the most likely reason for James to commission Robertson in preference to Ross to alter and renovate his mansion at Letham Grange on the estate in Angus which he had purchased in 1877.

John Robertson had been employed by Ross for over twenty years in the offices at 42 Union Street, Inverness but, on the strength of this very considerable assignment, he left this employment in 1880, crossed to the opposite side of the road to 39 Union Street and established himself in business. The offices at 39 had previously been occupied by the architects, Alexander and William Reid of Elgin and Inverness and with John Rhind also based at 3 Union Street, this street could well be considered the "Avenue of Architects."

In his first three years of self-employment, John Robertson was responsible for at least seventeen residences in the Inverness and surrounding area. At Fortrose in the Black Isle, he received

16. Fortrose Drill Hall by John Robertson 1881.
K. *MacLennan*.

ADVERTISEMENTS.

THE FORTROSE
VOLUNTEER HALL.

THIS Commodious Building, seated for 400, with PLATFORM and RETIRING ROOMS, can be hired at the following

SCALE OF CHARGES,
VIZ.:—

CONCERTS—First Night	£1 1	0
,, —Second Night	0 10	6
SOCIAL and POLITICAL MEETINGS	1 1	0
LECTURES and RELIGIOUS MEETINGS ...	0 10	6
BALLS	1 11	6

OTHER PURPOSES—SPECIAL ARRANGEMENTS.

Gas and Fire extra, according to Consumption.

AVAILABLE FOR THE USE OF

EXCURSION AND PIC-NIC PARTIES

FOR A SMALL CHARGE.

JANITOR'S FEE, 1/6 PER NIGHT, PAID BY PARTIES ENGAGING HALL.

Parties Engaging Hall responsible for Damage done.

THE CHARGES PAYABLE IN ADVANCE TO

MAJOR D. JACK, V.D.,
VOLUNTEER ORDERLY ROOM,
FORTROSE.

17. Advertisement for the hire of the Drill Hall.
Illustrated Guide to the Black Isle Railway
by A.J. Beaton, F.S.A. SCOT.

commissions for the Drill Hall, the Free Church manse and additions to a house known as the Priory. Included in his works in the Black Isle during this three year period was Kincurdie house and stables offices at Rosemarkie and the Station Hotel at Muir of Ord. He was, of course, also very occupied at Letham Grange, which in hindsight may have been an over-ambitious commission to have accepted for a first sole assignment, particularly with one as fastidious as James. With so many pressures bearing on him at one time, John's health showed signs of suffering under the strain.

An incident at Letham Grange involving James Fletcher did not improve the situation. The improvements and alterations were progressing satisfactorily until the building of the new tower was reached. A quote from the book "A Prospect of Sutherland" relates the incident:

"James Fletcher, when having a tower added to his house of Letham Grange, in Angus, was very exacting in his demands and if it was not to his liking simply told his builders to "Tak it doon." The tower was taken down and rebuilt several times."

John Robertson retired from the works at Letham Grange leaving James Fletcher with a potentially embarrassing situation that led him to approach John Rhind at the other end of Union Street, Inverness to complete the work.

It would seem that it took some time for Robertson to recover from his ill health. From the end of 1882 to the beginning of 1888 he completed very few commissions but the situation did improve and, as a specialist in church design, the years from 1890 to 1900 were his most fruitful, building or renovating numerous churches and church halls as well as residences in an area ranging from the east to the west of the Highlands. Fortrose Academy in the Black Isle was one of the few, if not the only school he designed. Building commenced in 1890 with additions being made in 1896.

The fourth child and second son of a large family, John Robertson never married and though he retired a considerable time

18. Fortrose Academy by John Robertson 1890.
Courtesy of Highland Council Archives, Inverness.

before his death in December 1925, he remained a familiar figure on the streets of Inverness, courteous, independent and "not without quaintness." His funeral cortege carried him from his home at Hawthornedean at Hill Place to the Old High Church of Scotland in Church Street where he was interred in the impressive 17th century Robertson of Inshes mausoleum situated to the right of the entrance gate. The weather and the passage of time have had a disastrous effect on the ornamental stonework of the rectangular monument. Sadly there is no inscription to mark the grave of John Robertson.

19. The Robertson of Inshes Mausoleum.
K. MacLeman.

JOHN RHIND

George Rhind, father of John, was a mason to trade when he married Isabella Milne in 1835 at Banff and it was here that John, the eldest of eight, was born in 1836. His birth was followed by that of another son, George, in 1837 and soon after the family moved to Inverness.

The father established a building and architectural business at 25 Castle Street in anticipation of his sons becoming involved. A third son, William, became a mason but John was sent to Glasgow to receive the best possible training in architecture. Of the three architects, Ross, Robertson and Rhind, John was the only one to receive formal training and, while in Glasgow, was much influenced by the style of Alexander "Greek" Thomson, the celebrated architect admired by architects for his inventive and controlled style and particularly for his designs in continuous street architecture.

During his training, John joined the Young Architects' Association of Glasgow and became its vice president. On his return to Inverness at the age of twenty-seven, he commenced his successful professional career, building a reputation as a leading designer in interior décor with overall use of the Scottish baronial style. In his third year alone his commitments extended in area from Skye to Oban to Inverness.

Though Alexander Ross was already well established in business in Inverness and was to receive many of the more notable commissions such as the Cathedral and the Bishop's Palace, John Rhind was no less successful, though his major works, which were frequently on country estates, were less evident to the general public.

From 1866 John's workload was impressive and recognition of his ability was gaining momentum. In 1869 he had no less than fourteen commissions ranging from Roy Bridge in the Lochaber district, to Kincraig in Badenoch and to Fortrose in the Black Isle.

Apart from the large volume of work, travelling such distances must have been exhausting in itself.

In 1870 the quality of his work came to the attention of Sir John William Ramsden, 5th Baronet of Yorkshire and Deputy Lieutenant of Inverness.

For many years James MacPherson was owner of the Ardverikie Estate in the Badenoch area but he leased it to the Duke of Abercorn for a lengthy period of time. The Duke had a house built there in 1836 and the white-washed walls of the rooms were decorated with murals painted by the celebrated artist Sir Edwin Landseer, already an acquaintance of the Duke. The most notable of these frescoes were titled "The Sanctuary", "The Challenge" and the most famous of all "The Monarch of the Glen."

Ardverikie House is situated on the edge of one of the finest inland lochs for trout fishing and the history of the area is associated with Pictish times when it was held sacred as the burial place of Caledonian Kings. Prior to her purchase of Balmoral, Queen Victoria visited Ardverikie with Prince Albert in 1847 during their quest for a Highland estate but it is reported that she considered the climate of the area over damp and wet.

Initially Sir John Ramsden acquired the tenancy from the Duke of Abercorn but became the owner of the estate in 1870. He was a man of great vigour and he gained much respect through his improvements on the estate which involved constructing miles of estate roads, planting forested areas and embarking on an extensive programme for the construction of houses for employees and the building of several shooting lodges.

John Rhind was commissioned to carry out alterations and additions to Ardverikie house and plans were drawn up in 1871. Unfortunately the mansion house was extensively damaged by fire in 1873 and tragically the Landseer frescoes were destroyed. The renovation plans were now a substantial undertaking but such a commission was a marvellous opportunity for John Rhind to display his considerable ability in interior design.

20. Ardverikie House by John Rhind 1871 - 78.
K. MacLeman.

21.
The turrets have contrasting stonework in a spiral effect.
K. MacLeman.

22. An example of the ornate ironwork surmounting the turrets.
K. MacLeman.

23. The walls of the main hall are clad in pitch pine with reeded and bound columns interrupting the strapped and studded panels.
K. MacLeman.

24. The richly carved oak panels in the hall were originally from Kensington Palace.
K. MacLeman.

25. An arch, which spans the width of the hall, is supported on composite pillars with marble stems. The plasterwork over the arch has a shield and foliage to the corners with an array of rosettes following the curve.

K. MacLeman.

26. One of several main doors leading from the hall.
K. MacLeman.

The few examples displayed here of his work at Ardverikie would seem to confirm this. It was 1878 before the works were completed.

The success of this work led to many more commissions not only on this estate but at Redcastle on the Black Isle and, in particular, at Moy, south of Inverness, where he was responsible for extensive additions and alterations to Moy Hall in 1872 and again in 1877. In 1879 he received instructions for the building of houses, offices, a stone bridge and a boathouse, all for the Ardverikie Estate. The Moy Estate also continued to make much use of his services.

During the years 1880 to 1882 John Rhind dealt with a gruelling workload but he was now suffering from emphysema of both lungs and was obviously not in good health. From 1882 onwards he barely managed to complete two commissions a year.

Though a skilled architect dedicated to his profession, John perhaps lacked the expertise of Alexander Ross in dealing with veteran businessmen. While holding the local office of Dean of Guild, questions were raised regarding John's position in a dispute which developed over plans for a new harbour office, the site of which was to be in the immediate vicinity of the Rhind family home at 2 Portland Place where John resided with his parents, brothers and sisters. As a person he was considered pleasant, agreeable and was a member of the High Church but such an accusation would have been greatly distressing to him.

John never married and with the death of his father in 1886 he, being the oldest son, doubtless felt it his responsibility to provide for his mother and those of his brothers and sisters who remained at home. On the 1st. of August 1889 he took the exceptional step of raising an action in court against Sir John Ramsden for approximately £2,000 due for various architectural services rendered during the years between 1871 and 1886. In the giving of evidence, the crux of the dispute centred on plans which may or may not have been drawn but for which estimated costs were so excessive that the works did not proceed. Towards the end of the second day of the hearing, it became clear to the Court that

John Rhind was not a well man and the Sheriff adjourned the proceedings until the following Monday, the 9th of August.

The trauma of the court case caused John to suffer insomnia and in the hope of recuperating he travelled to Perth during the adjournment. He died at Perth on the 10th of August 1889 at the age of 53, suffering from mental exhaustion as well as congestion of the lungs. His well-attended funeral moved to Tomnahurich Cemetery where he was interred alongside his father and younger brother, William.

27. John Rhind - 1836 to 1889.
K. MacLeman.

With regard to Letham Grange, John Robertson drew the plans for the major alterations in 1880 and commenced supervision of the construction. John Rhind completed the works with changes and was responsible for the interior décor, while Alexander Ross was employed by Fitzroy Fletcher in 1887 to make further minor improvements.

28. Lochardil mansion house by John Rhind 1876.
K. MacLeman.

29. Inverness High Public School by John Rhind 1878.
K. MacLeman.

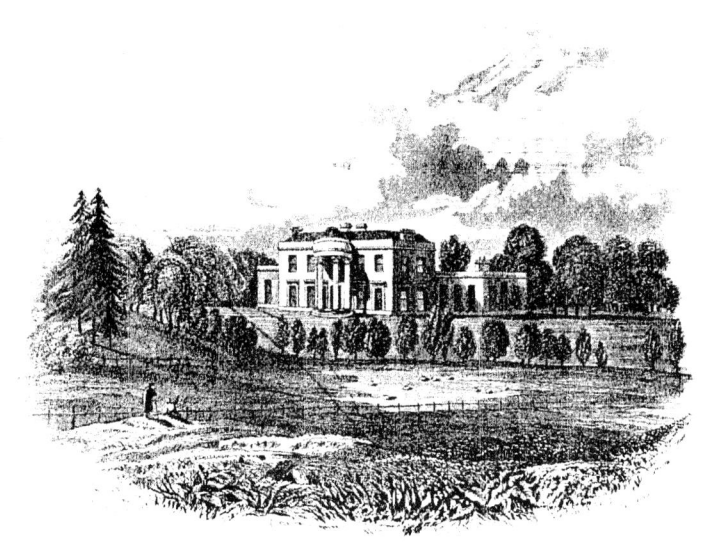

30. Letham Grange by Archibald Simpson 1827.

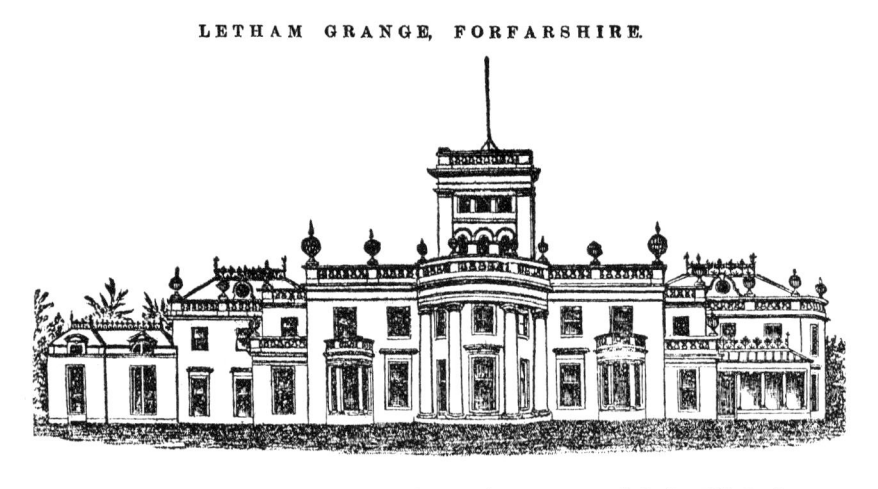

31. Letham Grange by John Robertson and John Rhind.
1880 to 1885.

The Mansion of Letham Grange.

Now in his seventies, James Fletcher perhaps saw Letham Grange as his last opportunity to use his wealth to great effect. In 1880, he presented John Robertson, a gifted draughtsman, but as yet an inexperienced architect from Inverness, with the considerable challenge of redesigning this classic house by the renowned Aberdeen architect Archibald Simpson. Archibald Simpson had designed plans in 1827 for John Hay, the owner at that time, but in the interceding years up to the time of James' purchase, the demands of the wealthy and the idiosyncrasies of society had greatly altered opinions regarding what was considered necessary in a "great" house. What had been appropriate for the limited demands of an unmarried country gentleman such as John Hay was no longer appropriate for a wealthy entrepreneur such as James Fletcher.

A splendid view of Letham Grange could be had from the Arbroath and Forfar Railway which bordered the grounds of the estate on the west side. The existing building was already one of great dimensions with an impressive portico of four classic pillars rising to two levels on the southwest façade, but James had a penchant for bay windows, stone balustrades and entrance porches, and these Letham Grange did not have in 1877 when he purchased it.

Whatever his self-indulgence, James was, whenever possible, a staunch supporter of local skilled men, and there was a blend of Inverness and Arbroath craftsmen at Letham Grange.

From Arbroath there were the firms of James Whyte for carpentry and joinery, Farquharson was the glazier, and the ironwork was made by George Anderson and Company. The fundamental plastering and cementing was completed by Alfred Guthrie of Dundee. The master masons of Harrow and Sinclair travelled from Inverness, as did John Tulloch of 48 Academy Street, Inverness: he was responsible for the painting and papering. The first superintendent of works was John Anderson but William Hay assumed this responsibility on the death of Anderson.

For the specialist tasks of ornate plasterwork, panelling and the marble fireplaces of the principal rooms, firms were employed from further afield. George Rome and Company of Glasgow and Dublin were responsible for the intricate plasterwork, and in later years they accomplished comparable work of an equally high standard at Ardmulchan for Fitzroy Fletcher. The firm of Wallace and Connell, who were the plumbers and lead merchants at Letham Grange, were also based in Glasgow at Argyle Street and at North Street in the Anderston district. For the oak, walnut and marble creations, James sought out Howard and Sons of London, a firm which had exhibited at the London Exhibition of 1862. Described as "upholsterers, decorators and cabinet makers", Howard and Sons were indeed well qualified to satisfy the demands of James Fletcher.

Through the castellated arch from the Colliston and Letham Grange road, an entry can be made to the policies and the mansion. In 1877 a long wooded drive led to the north approach of the house.

The employment of greater numbers of servants, the provision of greater catering facilities, coupled with the dictates of fashionable foibles for more public rooms to fulfil the different social functions, all presented John Robertson with the dilemma of providing this extra space without despoiling the lines of the existing building. His solution was to add wings to the northeast and southeast corners and their projections from the original wall afforded the main entrance the suggestion of a courtyard.

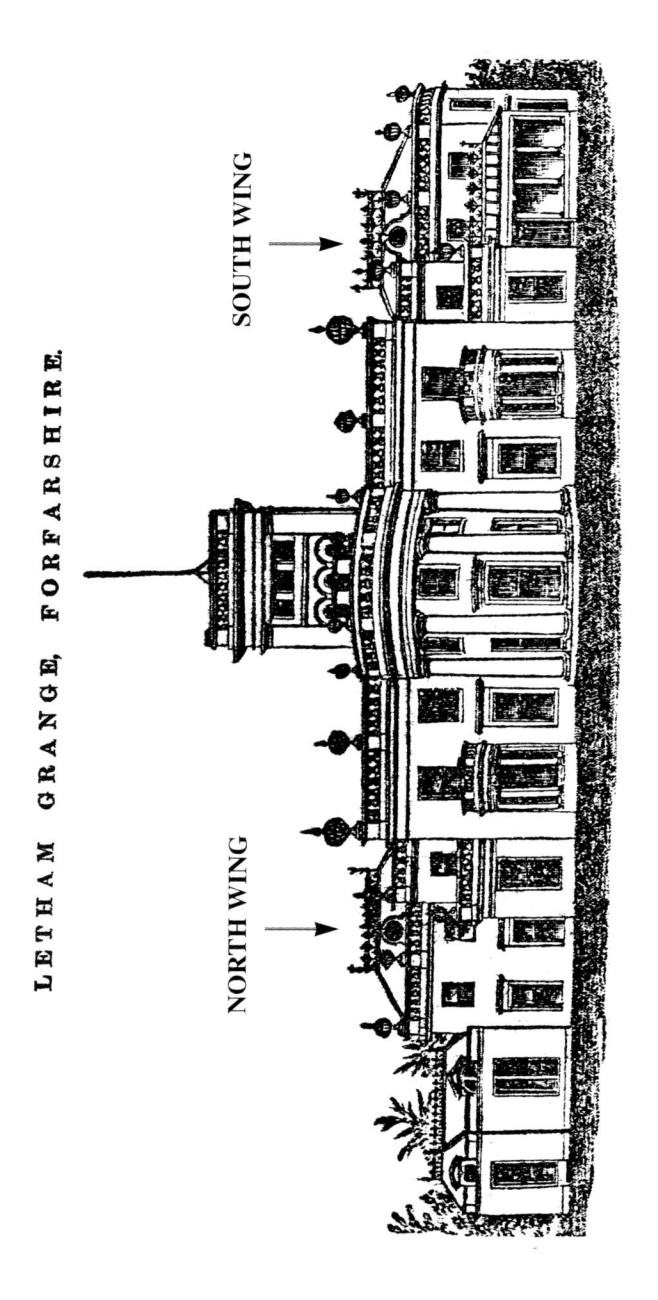

32. A drawing of Letham Grange - circa 1885.

33. The tower of Letham Grange.
K. MacLeman.

This entrance has a central position between the additional wings and the appended stone porch projects from the original main wall. Tuscan columns, to match those of the southern portico, flank this front opening and the corners of the balustraded parapet are supported on pilasters which are crowned with classic urns. A decorative balustraded parapet surmounts the outer walls of the entire house, including the new wings, the tower and the additional bay windows. There is a profusion of classic urns at the upper parapet level, placed strategically for maximum effect but mainly on the south and west perimeters. The roofs of both wings have been garnished with elaborate wrought iron railings set above the "porthole" style of windows which light what was the staff bedrooms in the attic areas.

With such embellishments to the house, John Robertson must surely have succeeded thus far in meeting the demands of James though it is unclear at what stage of the construction Robertson became ill. It is generally accepted that much of the exterior work had been completed while he was still directing operations. John Rhind may have been responsible for the roof embellishments but he was certainly not involved in the infamous "Tak it doon" tower. This square tower was reached by metal spiral stairs which ascended from outside bedroom three. It contained two levels with access to a balcony above the portico which gave a spectacular panoramic outlook on to surrounding landscape. It must remain conjecture as to whether James was satisfied or not with the final result but the top of the tower seems somewhat blunt. The four corners appear to lack a finishing touch - perhaps four classic urns! John Rhind assumed responsibility from this point and designed the interior decorations.

Changes are essential for the survival of any building, and so it was at Letham Grange. The 1970s floor plans of R.W. Ritchie and Dick, architects of Brechin, were drawn in preparation for a planning application to alter Letham Grange to an hotel. Their proposals were superimposed on an earlier set of plans, but since there is no signature it is impossible to attribute these earlier plans to any one architect.

By utilising the plans of R.W. Ritchie and Dick, an effort has been made, for the purpose of reference, to revert to the original layout for each level of the building.

A short passage with doors at each end connects the spacious front porch to the hall, an arrangement which would have had a great impact on arriving guests, with the welcoming host in position in the hall.

34. The main entrance of Letham Grange.
K. MacLeman.

At this point the hall divides to the left and to the right. At the end of the right divide, there is a door leading to the north wing which contained the utilitarian area. This part was almost exclusively the servants' and service area excepting one room, the gunroom, which had a curved window overlooking the main entrance. The position of the butler's pantry served to emphasise his importance in the household: all the movements of the staff to the main parts of the house were scrutinised by him as they passed through his room. Opposite his pantry, there was a door leading to the still room where he would have decanted the port for dinner.

When drawing the plans, Robertson had to consider the arrangements of all the rooms so that they would reflect a residence appropriate to the social standing of his clients. The utility offices of a large house were a necessity, the existence of which Victorian owners did not care to acknowledge. It was especially crucial that cooking odours did not penetrate to the family's rooms: the kitchen was therefore situated distant from the family area, through numerous doors and with little regard to the problem of serving food hot.

At the end of the long corridor which ran the length of the north wing, there was a rear entrance from the covered court. It was used by the servants to come and go without being visible to either the owners or guests but it was also used by the gentlemen when returning from a shooting excursion.

35. The area opposite the rear door when it was in use for displaying hunting trophies.
Courtesy of Private Collection.

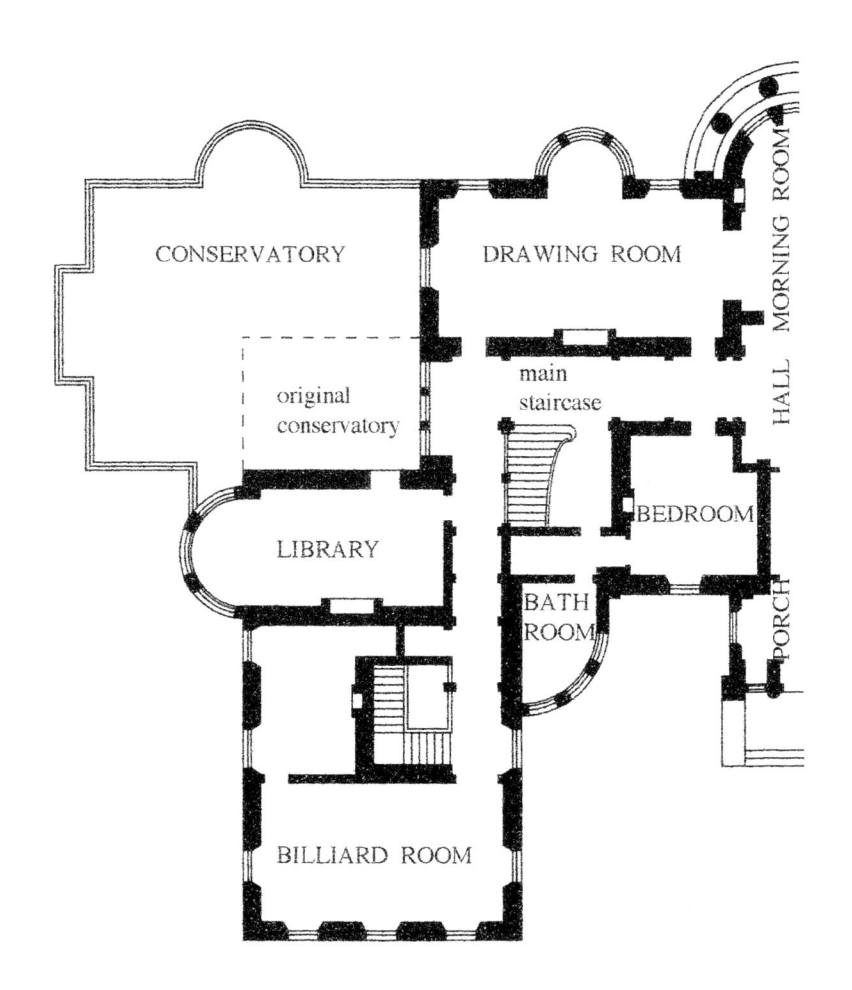

LETHAM GRANGE
Ground Floor Plan

36a. Ground Floor Plan as circa 1885.

36b. Ground Floor Plan as circa 1885.

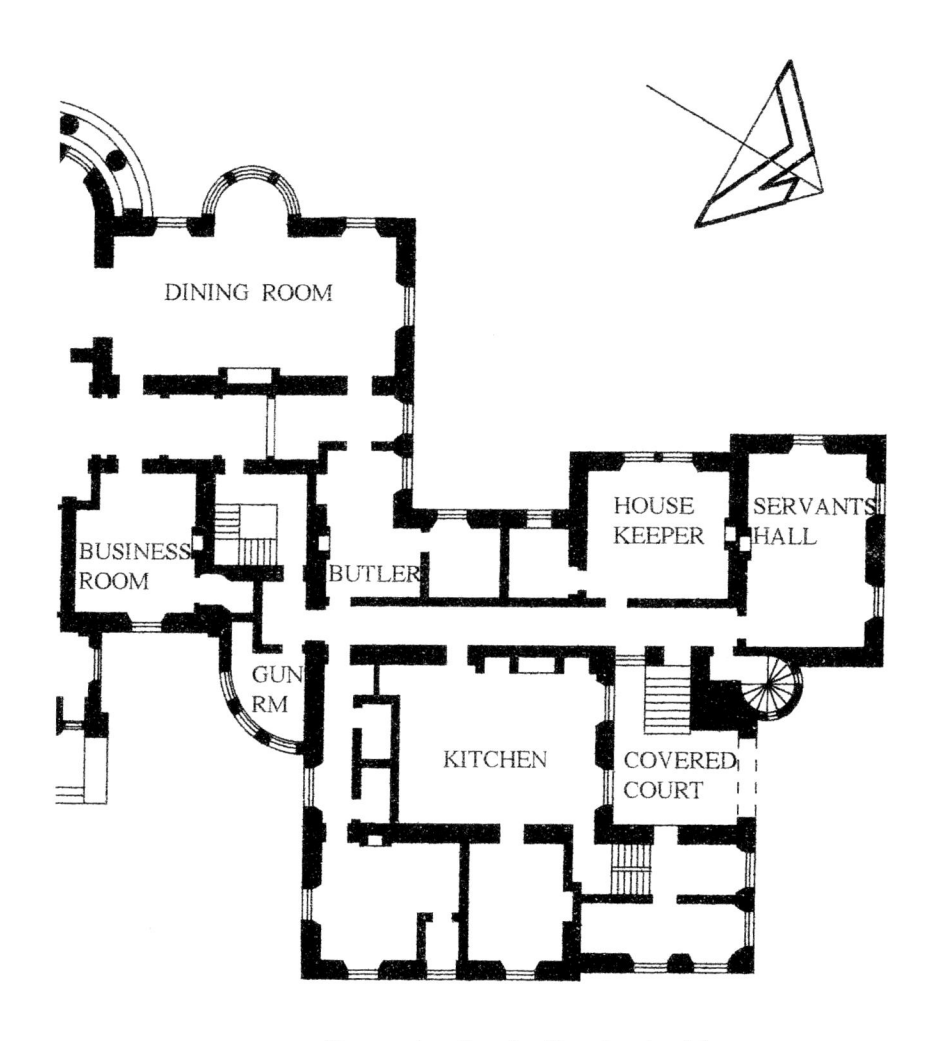

Drawn by Sandy Gracie, Architect
from plans by R W Ritchie & Dick, Brechin

This north wing had a servants' hall and between it and the butler's room there was an area noted on the plans as "private rooms", the function of which would seem to have changed over the years. On the plans of the period circa 1880, it is noted as a housekeeper's room. Alexander Ross carried out further alterations for Fitzroy Fletcher in 1887 and with Fitzroy's interest in hunting and shooting, and with the proximity of this area to the gunroom, it became a male domain for the displaying of trophies from successful hunting trips. (See No. 35.)

Next to the rear entrance was a spiral staircase which descended to the valet's room in the basement and rose to the first floor level where a series of doors and corridors provided the valet with access to the bedrooms; this enabled him to deliver suitably polished shoes or to aid the gentlemen to dress. At the opposite side of the courtyard, there was a vegetable preparation room and store. There appears, however, to have been an omission from this utilitarian part - a laundry.

On returning to the main hall, there are two small rooms on either side of the front door. On the later plans they are shown as a sitting room and a small dining room, both of which would have served a practical purpose in cold weather when there were no guests, but according to the wishes of James they were to be a bedroom and business room. (See No. 36a. & 36b.)

The morning room was placed immediately opposite the front door and between the drawing room and the dining room. The bay of this room repeats the curve of the columns of the portico and the windows have been positioned to make a view possible between the rise of these columns. An opening of nine feet incorporates the door from the hall and consists of four sections containing glass panels set in wood with turned brass columns fixed behind the glass. Below, is a fretwork of arched columns and carved wooden panels. This whole feature has been referred to as the "bird cage". The ceiling of this room is of a richly moulded plasterwork with an overlay of ornamentation while a deep gilded frieze displays the fruits of the Greek gods.

37. The ornate doorway of the Morning Room.
K. MacLeman.

The "morning room" measures approximately twenty-four feet by sixteen feet and the folding doors on either side are nine feet in width. This permitted the convenient option of combining all three rooms if required for the "grand" occasion. Oak panelling covers the lower part of the walls.

To the right lay the dining room, named later as the "Rosehaugh Room" after James' estate in the Black Isle, and here, as in the drawing room, one of the bay windows much favoured by James was added. Oak was used throughout this room. The high dado has a border of intricately carved trailing foliage with birds, hares and dogs discreetly introduced at intervals in the foliage. The ceiling is lined with oak and the ribbed decoration gives an overall baronial hall effect. The ribbing continues into the centre pendant where there is a profusion of carved oak leaves, and twin cherubs' heads have been added to each of the outer segments.

A newspaper cutting of the time described the chimneypiece as, ***"richly carved, the jambs being formed of caryatides which support a heavily moulded overmantel."*** In the early photograph shown, the caryatides, which are carved female supports, have disappeared along with the overmantel which had been replaced with a large portrait of James Fletcher, the portrait which now hangs in the main stairwell. In the modern photograph, the chimneypiece has been replaced with one similar to the original, and caryatides are again in place.

When Fitzroy became owner, the large public rooms would have been occupied only in the summer months. The gentry followed a busy and much travelled itinerary during the calendar year. Their absence from census returns carried out routinely in April every ten years can be accounted for - it was the time of year when they resided in the south of France or travelled the colonies. The large houses were then usually closed and left in the charge of a housekeeper and one other servant. The calendar of the social classes was based on being at specific venues at specific times. The family would return in June to enjoy whatever pleasant weather there would be and remain for the best of the grouse and pheasant season.

38. The Dining Room - circa 1900.
Courtesy of Private Collection.

39. The fireplace of the Dining Room.
K. MacLeman.

Depending on personal preferences, there were variations during the months of October to March: for those who leased or owned a town house, the festive season would be spent in London at the theatre, at the many balls and enjoying social visits; others, like Fitzroy, ignored the London "scene" and went visiting to the estates of friends or acquaintances for the sport of hunting.

40. The ceiling pendant of the Dining Room.
K. MacLeman.

The dimensions of the drawing room were equal to that of the dining room - approximately thirty-seven feet by eighteen feet. These measurements did not include the area of the bay window which amounted to ten feet across by seven feet deep. Of the front public rooms, the drawing room would have been the most pleasant, a show-piece receiving the maximum amount of sunlight, and it is to this room that the ladies withdrew after dinner, leaving the gentlemen to the serious drinking and questionable conversation. From this aspect, it was well placed. The position of the morning room between the dining room and the drawing room would have prevented the ladies from hearing any uncouth language!

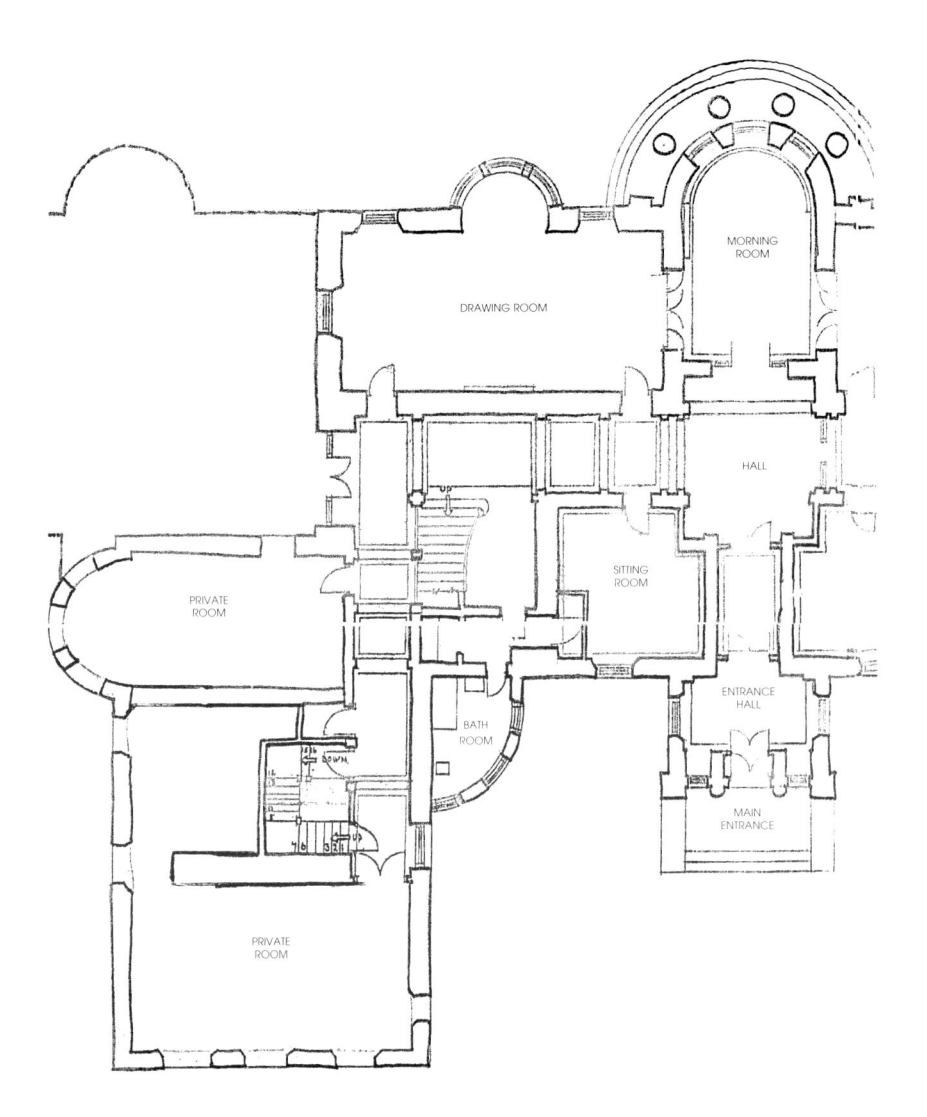

41. The south section of Letham Grange House - circa 1887. Adjustments made from the plans of Ritchie and Dick by K. MacLeman.

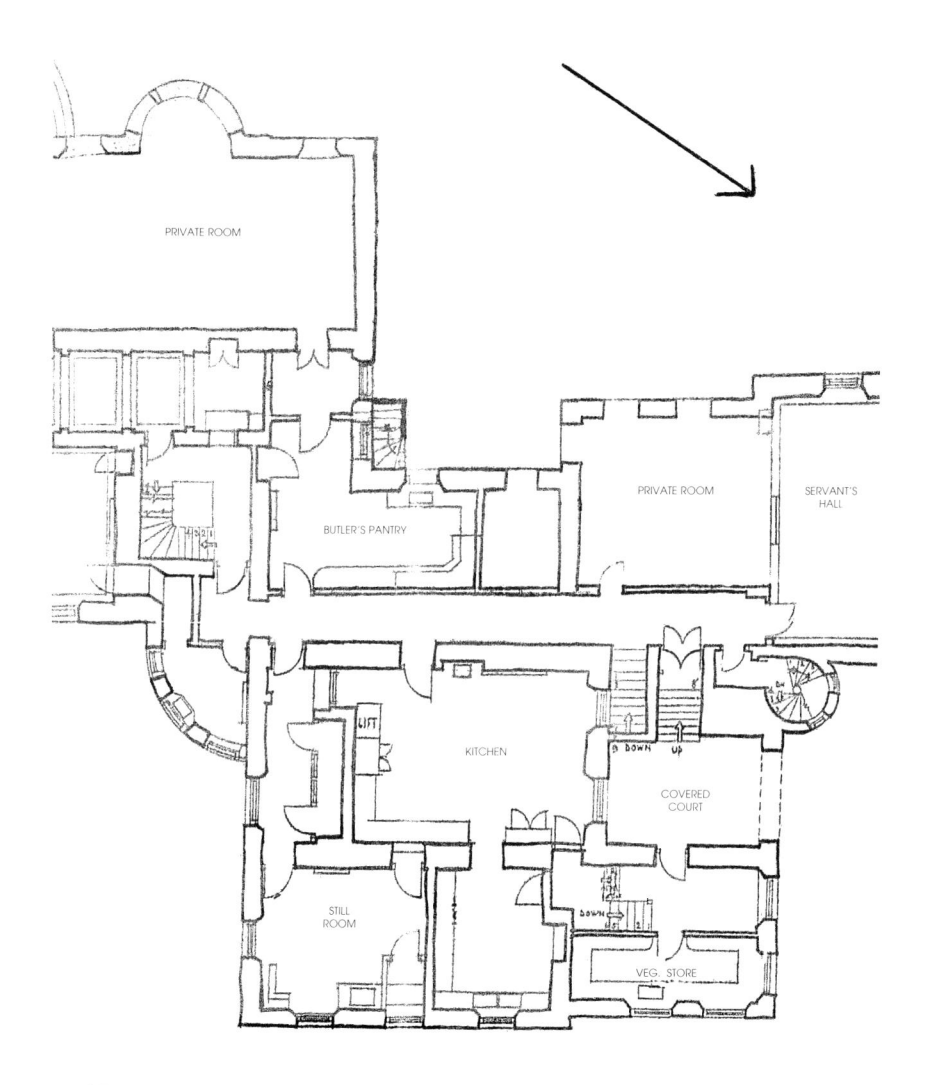

42. The north section of Letham Grange House - circa 1887.
Adjustments made from the plans of Ritchie and Dick
by K. MacLeman.

The original fireplace of the drawing room remains in place and the carved walnut surround glows with a rich patina. The grooved marble insert contrasts with the walnut, and the beaten metal panels on either side of the hearth are not only practical but also effective. There was no overmantel in place in the past and the walls were decorated with a flocked paper from below a deep gilded frieze which has since been removed; this frieze had matched that of the frieze now in the morning room. The drawing room ceiling is composed of richly moulded paper-hanging work overlaid with a decoration in a Greek style. The overall impression is that it would have been a pleasant and comfortable room despite its size.

43. The fireplace of the Drawing Room.
K. MacLeman.

44. The Drawing Room circa 1900.
Courtesy of Private Collection.

45. Detail of cornice in Drawing Room.
K. MacLeman.

46. One of the wide doorways between the public rooms.
K. MacLeman.

In the corridor outside the door at the south end of the drawing room, there was an opening into the conservatory, the conservatory which was later replaced by Fitzroy. This later and more extensive one was of a steel structure: it covered the south window of the drawing room and extended to align with the outer southwest wall of the house. The rear wall of the conservatories was common with the library which had a doorway directly into the conservatory as well as access to the corridor. Great importance was attached to the library of a house and it was used on occasions by guests who did not wish to drink or to mingle with the ladies in the drawing room. On this occasion, the library was equipped with pitch pine bookcases inlaid with ebony in a classic style.

47. The inside of the 1885 Conservatory.
Courtesy of Private Collection.

At ground level, the southeast wing provided the accommodation for the library, a servants' stair and a spacious billiard room. Situated between the library and the billiard room, and with access from the billiard room only, was a smoking room.

48. Letham Grange with conservatory built for Fitzroy Fletcher. Photograph by Anckorn of Arbroath circa 1900. *Courtesy of Private Collection.*

These rooms were a male domain yet the double entrance doors to the billiard room are the most ornate and impressive in the house. Measuring thirty-two feet by eighteen feet, the room is panelled to more than three-quarters of the height of the walls and has a plaster ceiling with a narrow gilt frieze immediately below. The large open fireplace has a tiled recess. The tiles display Indian or Middle Eastern men on horseback and may have been a later addition by Fitzroy, exhibiting his interest in horses. These tiles are not entirely in harmony with the stone jambs and carved lintels of the fireplace. Fixed to the wall and within easy reach of the billiard table, was a voice mouthpiece, an essential for the gentlemen when the after-dinner brandy had been consumed. A request for a replenishing of supplies could be made direct to the butler's pantry by means of this equipment.

49. The voice piece in the Billiard Room.
K. MacLeman.

The corridor which connects the billiard room door with that of the drawing room, runs parallel with the first flight of the main stairs. Light is received from the roof-light above the stairwell and so through the openings between columns. The left hand stretcher and balustrade of the stairs sweeps in a graceful inward curve and the ornate balustrade continues round a walk-way

50. The fireplace of the Billiard Room.
K. MacLeman.

51. The doorway of the Billiard Room.
K. MacLeman.

52. The main stairs. *K. MacLeman.*

53. The portrait of James Fletcher in the stairwell. *K. MacLeman.*

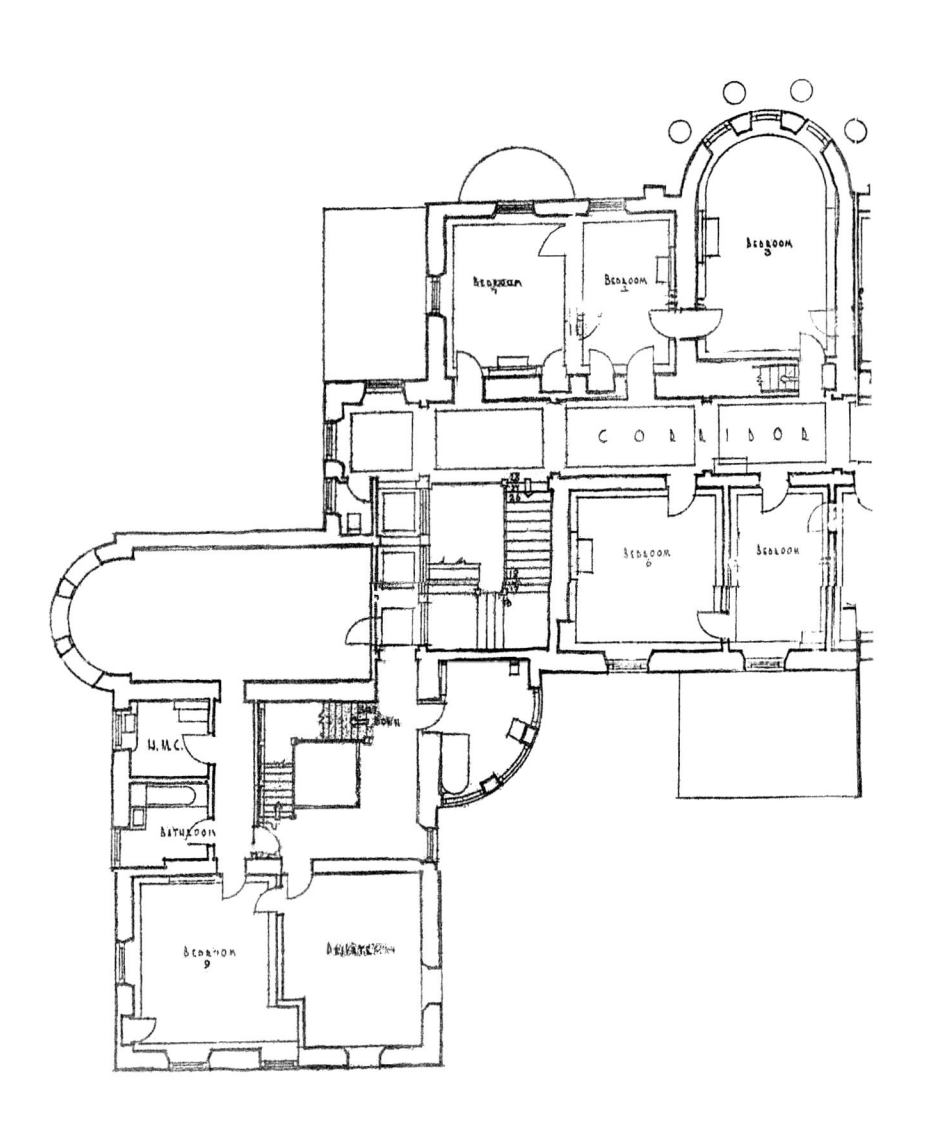

54. The south section of the first floor - circa 1887.
Adjustments made from the plans of Ritchie and Dick
by K. MacLeman.

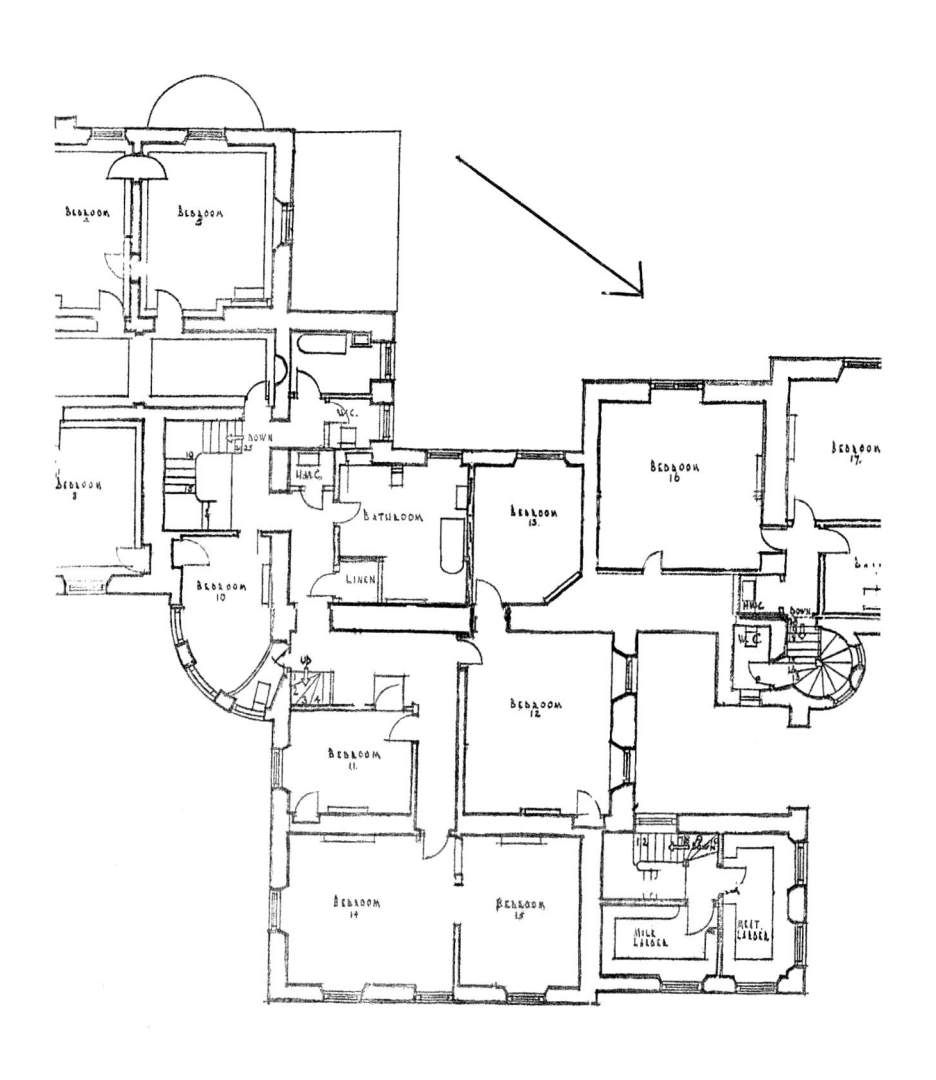

55. The north section of the first floor - circa 1887.
Adjustments made from the plans of Ritchie and Dick
by K. MacLeman.

on the first floor, only interrupted by the rise of the ground floor columns which culminate above in arches.

The first floor accommodated the guests' bedrooms and the most superior of these were ranged above the bay windows and portico. Many bedrooms had communicating doors, with the smaller room in each case serving as a dressing room if required. Immediately outside the door to bedroom three, a narrow staircase led up to the tower. At the north end of this corridor, there was a bathroom and separate water closet discreetly placed beyond a door and through an alcove, a position in keeping with Victorian attitudes. The three bedrooms on the opposite side of the corridor and above the front entrance and would have served as accommodation for guests of secondary importance or for important servants accompanying guests.

56. The first floor corridor to the right of the stairs.
Taken outside Bedroom No. 3, circa 1900.
Courtesy of Private Collection.

There were four bathrooms on this floor for guests and a housemaid's cupboard at either end. In 1880, the number of baths installed in a house was in relation to the amount of money made available by the owner. James was not without adequate funds and could well have provided baths for every bedroom, but a quote from an 1880 book would seem to be relevant: *"It is a common error to suppose that persons of ample means have no need to be economical. It is precisely where there are the most means that economy is the greatest virtue; for, without reasonable regard for economy, the rich must speedily become poor."*

Bedrooms were frequently used as a retreat for privacy, private reading or for writing letters and suitable furniture for these purposes was provided. In later years the family used a large area to the left at the top of the main stairway in preference to the downstairs library. This upper part was infinitely warmer in the winter months.

The second floor was of two unrelated sections on top of the newly-added wings. All had combe-ceilings and were the staff bedrooms. Coal fires were provided in all except one but neither a bath nor a water closet was fitted in the south-east section. The servants in the north-east wing had a bath only, but as it had no fire it must have been a thought to contemplate having a bath in the middle of winter when the frost could be scraped off the window panes - on the inside! The coal fires were only lit in the event of illness or on special occasions. A lenient employer may well allow one to be lit in severe weather conditions or have left it to the discretion of the housekeeper. With regard to chimneys, the 1880 book states: *"It is unlawful for any person to be a party to any child or young person ascending or descending a chimney for the purpose of sweeping, cleaning or for extinguishing fire therein."* The penalty for the guilty was ten pounds or six months with hard labour!

There would appear to have been only one staff toilet, situated on the bend of the spiral stairs between the ground and first floors on the north wing. All guest and staff bedrooms would, of

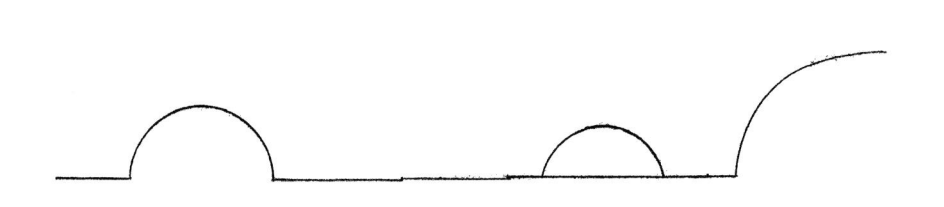

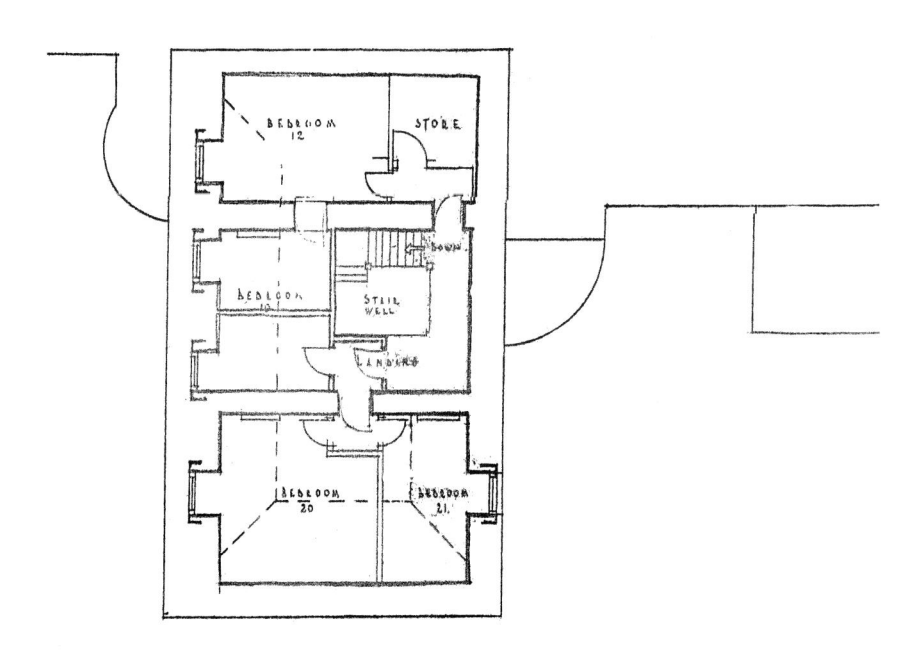

57. The top floor of the south section.
Adjustments made from the plans of Ritchie and Dick
by K. MacLeman.

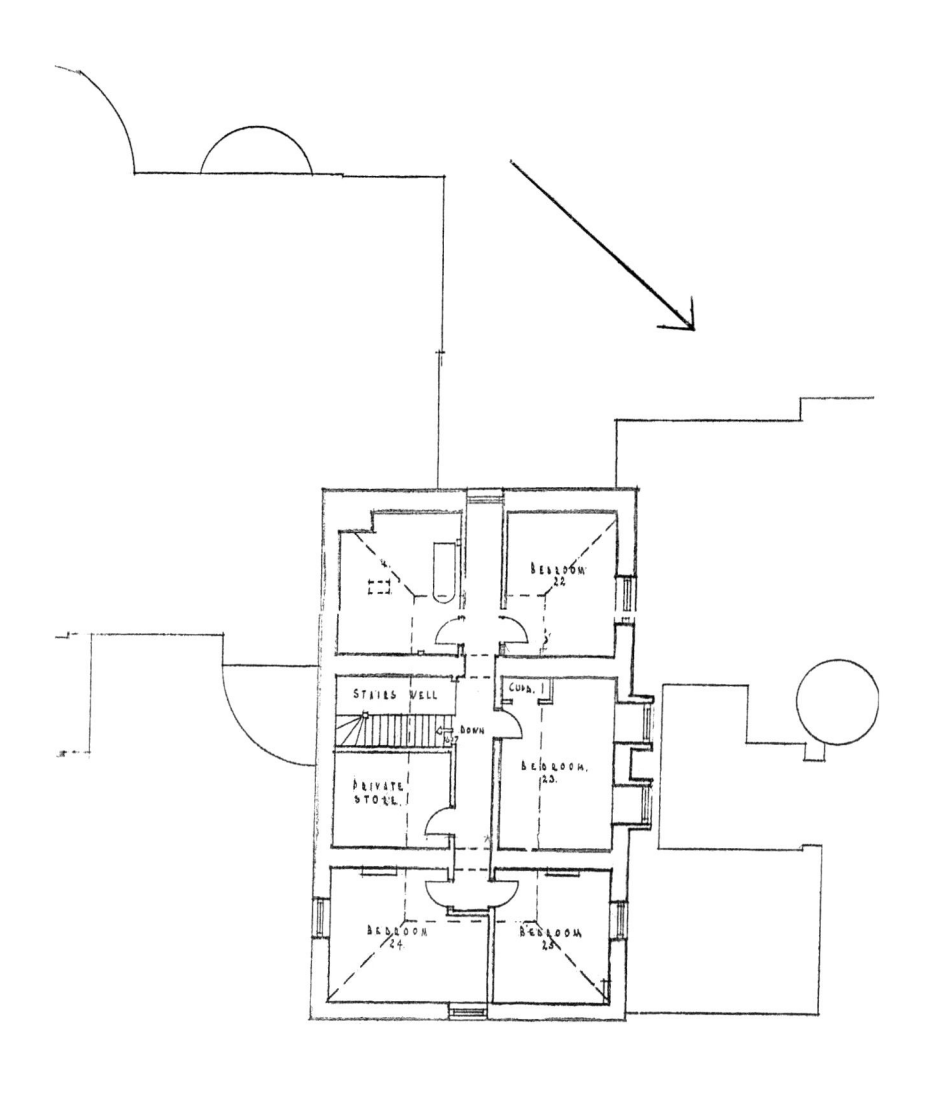

58. The top floor of the north section.
Adjustments made from the plans of Ritchie and Dick
by K. MacLeman.

course, have ewer and basin sets for washing and these sets included the essential chamber pot for emergencies.

The basement level can be seen in relation to the perimeter outline of the main part of the house. A service staircase close to the owner's private rooms on the ground floor gave access to the basement as well as to the first floor. The fuel store and wine cellars were reached by a long corridor, but fuel was delivered through a chute situated to the right of the front door. A furnace room housed a hot - water steam boiler, a heating boiler and a caloridier and these boilers heated the building by circulating hot water through cast iron pipes. Fitted in 1885, this heating system must have been envied by many of the guests.

This part of the basement could also be accessed from another stair in the north wing, identical to the other, and which descended from outside the butler's pantry. The layout meant that, on a command from the billiard room through the voice-piece, the butler could descend to the wine cellars to collect replenishments for the gentlemen and mount by the stairs outside the billiard room. The servants supplied the requirements of the family and guests by the use of the stairs in each wing; on no occasion would they use the main staircase. There was an external staircase on the north side for deliveries of meat to the basement.

In the north wing, there was a separate and unconnected section below ground floor level containing the valet's room and a beer cellar which was situated immediately below the kitchen. A connecting lift to the kitchen eased the burden of transportation. These lower parts were also reached by stone steps near the servants' entrance.

The management of these mansions was very labour intensive. The fetching and carrying of water, the lighting and cleaning of so many coal fires, the cleaning of so many rooms and the sheer volume of laundering and ironing without the benefits of modern appliances meant an early rising and a day of no relaxation for the house-maids.

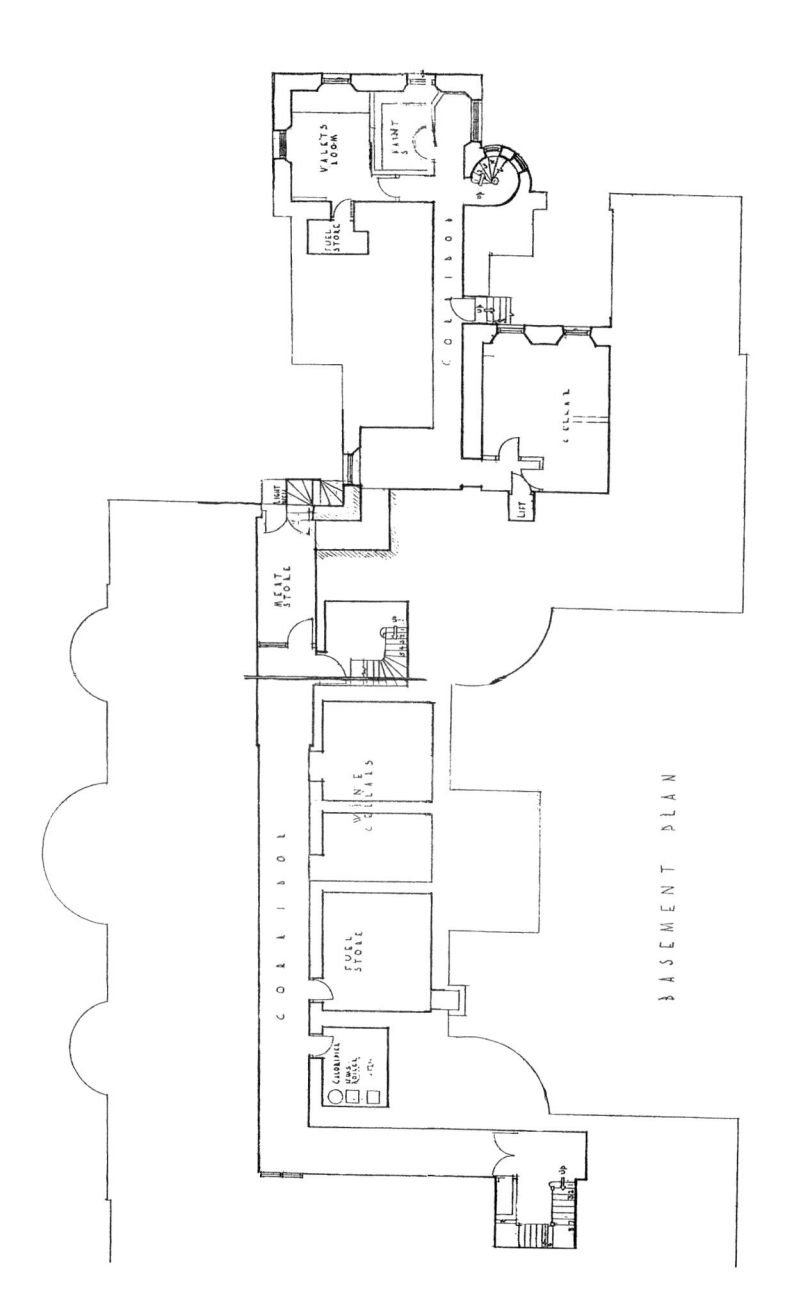

59. Basement floor. Adjustments made from the plans of Ritchie & Dick by K. MacLeman.

From the plans, it can be seen that there was an addition to the north wing extension, unbalancing the symmetry of the north and south wings. This extra space provided two bedrooms and a bathroom for the butler and the housekeeper and below, there was the servants' hall.

For John Rhind, the interior decorating of Letham Grange would have been another great opportunity for him to exercise his particular abilities; but in contrast to the freedom he enjoyed at Ardverikie, James Fletcher would have maintained a watchful eye. The décor of all the main public rooms and the balustrade of the stairs exhibit clearly the designs of John Rhind. The house was completed though not furnished in 1885, barely days before the death of James on the first of October.

As there is no available information regarding the changes made by Alexander Ross at Letham Grange in 1887, one can only ponder as to what they may have been. At this time, Fitzroy was introducing many innovative ideas on the estate and, apart from installing electricity in the house, he would doubtless have had other concepts for changes. It is not inconceivable that the plans used by R.W. Ritchie and Dick may have been drawn in the offices of Alexander Ross.

60. Letham Grange in the 1990s.
K. MacLeman.

61. Fitzroy Charles Fletcher.
Courtesy of Private Collection.

FITZROY CHARLES FLETCHER

At almost thirty years of age, Fitzroy was unmarried, tall, handsome and the wealthy owner of Letham and Fern Estates with a preference for the more relaxed pace of life in the country rather than the lively pace of London. A young lady, who occasionally visited Letham Grange with her aunt, was Miss Ellaline Terriss, an accomplished and very beautiful London actress who excelled in the varying roles she played. Some expected the friendship with Fitzroy to develop to a union, but Miss Terriss was an enthusiastic part of the London social scene and, though appreciative of Fitzroy's friendship, could not envisage herself in the role of landowner's wife in "remote" Scotland. She later married Sir Seymour Hicks but she remained friends with Fitzroy and continued to visit Fern Estate for the shooting season.

Being a local landowner of substantial means, Fitzroy was expected to become involved in local affairs. The years from 1885 to 1890 were busy years for him but, for one of a reserved temperament, it was a difficult task to emulate the supremacy of his father. Fitzroy's generous and concerned manner, however, soon endeared him to the local population. He was a local Justice of the Peace, a member of the County Council for Fern Parish and also for Arbroath and St Vigeans Parish and County Councils. Having shrewd business capabilities, he was considered well qualified for these positions. He was also a great supporter of the Arbroath Infirmary and other local benevolent institutions. Though never actively concerned with politics, he was on occasion asked to speak in support of Conservative candidates, and he proved that he possessed an ability as a public speaker, knowledgeable in local and world events.

62. Miss Ellaline Terriss.
By A.P.P.S. Ltd. Rickmansworth.
Courtesy of Private Collection.

63. Frances Mary Grant - later Fletcher.
Courtesy of Private Collection.

Whereas James Fletcher had greatly enlarged and virtually reconstructed the mansion house at Letham Grange, Fitzroy continued the completion of the renovation work by spending lavishly on improvements on the home farm and in enhancing the policies and grounds surrounding the house. The similarities between developments at Letham Grange with those which took place at Rosehaugh, the home of Fitzroy's brother James Douglas Fletcher, are such that there must have been detailed discussions and exchange of ideas between the brothers, with several of the innovations being first executed at Letham Grange.

While in Australia on family business, Fitzroy met Frances Mary, daughter of James MacPherson Grant and former wife of Francis Sidney Stephen, grandson of Sidney, Supreme Judge of New Zealand. Fitzroy was greatly attracted to her and the acquaintanceship blossomed, culminating in a marriage in 1890 at the Crown Court Church, the Strand, London witnessed by Fitzroy's brother James Douglas, and by Frances Mary's mother, Mary Grant. Frances Mary settled at Letham Grange with two sons from her previous marriage, Conway and Thomas, aged ten and eight. Attractive, vivacious and fashionable, she adopted the role of Laird's wife with ease and was popular with those who managed local affairs.

At the same time that he inherited the Letham Grange Estate, Fitzroy also inherited the Fern Estate which was situated north-east of Forfar and was of rolling countryside, wooded and well cultivated. This estate provided the terrain for grouse and pheasant shooting and for stalking deer. As the moors at Fern were ranked amongst the best in the Country, Fitzroy had an extra large and imposing shooting lodge built - Shandford Lodge. Guests, invited for the season, could not have failed to be impressed, not only with the grandeur of the building but also with the setting and spectacular views.

64. Shandford Lodge, Fern built for Fitzroy Fletcher.
K. MacLeman.

65. A stone tablet inserted in the front wall of Shandford Lodge bears the initials of Fitzroy Charles Fletcher.
K. MacLeman.

66. In anticipation of a successful day's shooting.
Courtesy of H. Gordon.

It was at Fern that one of the important local occasions required the presence of Frances Mary. The laying of the foundation stone for Fern Public Library took place on the first of October 1897, a date which coincided with the Jubilee celebrations of Queen Victoria's 60 years' reign. James Fletcher had always extolled the importance of education but had appreciated that it still remained a luxury for many families in spite of the 1875 Education Act. He had provided encouragement for gifted pupils through bursaries and Fitzroy continued this tradition by donating the new Fern Library which was sited in close proximity to the school and the church and was also to serve for other local recreational purposes. James Stirling, the estate master of works, had prepared the plans and was to supervise the construction.

A luncheon for a hundred and forty persons was held in a loft at Shandford Farm on Fern Estate and after a sumptuous meal and gratifying toasts, the company removed to the site where they were joined by other invited guests of Fitzroy - Mr Gradwell from County Meath, Mr A T Kent, Mr W Nevett and Captain Deuvaux, London. Dr. Ferguson opened the proceedings, referring to Fitzroy as a warm-hearted and open-handed proprietor who had made the residents of Fern Parish the envy of the whole country. Though they had not known Mrs Fletcher for as long as they had known Mr Fletcher, he said, ***"The more we know Mrs Fletcher, the more we like her."*** Only the week before, she had displayed much kindness and generosity in providing a handsome and magnificent organ for the Church.

For the ceremony Frances Mary was presented with a silver and inscribed trowel with an ivory handle. Once a bottle containing current coins and various documents was placed in the cavity, the foundation stone was lowered amidst loud cheers. Mr Nicoll of Hilton stated in a speech that he had known Mr Fletcher for fifteen years during which time he had always shown himself liberal and generous, ever ready to give a portion of the means with which he had been blessed to promote the welfare of others. Mr Nicoll continued that Fitzroy had carried on the good works begun by his father. Fern Estate had been in a most ruinous state when bought by James but they not only had a beautiful new Church but all farmhouses, steadings and bothies had been now greatly improved and, in addition, they were to have a library where they could improve their minds and enjoy an occasional dance.

Fitzroy replied with his thanks for Mr Nicoll's kind words and spoke of his hopes for the uses of the building where the library was to be free. He concluded by stating how much Mrs Fletcher had enjoyed her summer at Fern and that she anticipated returning for many more. The festivities continued late into the evening.

At a later stage in the construction of the Library, a stone tablet bearing a Latin inscription was inserted in the gable wall. The stone had been hewn from the estate quarry and carved by the estate masons.

67. Stone tablet bearing Latin inscription, Fern Library.
K. MacLeman.

Translations of Latin inscriptions can vary slightly but the sentiment is the same.

"The 60th year of Victoria's Reign.
The year is optimistic that the years may also spare the building.
The inscription is silent about all those who are modest.
We have three requests - Wisdom each year for those who learn.
Dancing each year for those weary with learning.
A happy teacher who teaches lessons to be remembered for many years.
May you be sweet, red Fern and long may you flourish.

1897"

68. Fern Library.
K. MacLeman.

The spacious grounds at Letham Grange provided the facilities for outdoor social occasions and with pleasant memories of his time spent in the regiment of the Scots Greys Fitzroy arranged a performance by their band at a garden party held at Letham Grange in July 1898. "The weather was indeed favourable and the large and fashionable company of assembled ladies and gentlemen thoroughly enjoyed the entertainment provided."

Though Fitzroy gained much enjoyment from the sport of shooting, his preferred pastime was the sport of hunting for which the land at Fern was unsuitable. A keen and able horseman, his passion resulted in the erection of fine, spacious and perfectly equipped stables and coachhouses at Letham Grange where a stud of racing horses was maintained.

His pleasure in the hunt led him to seek suitable territory elsewhere and through friendships he received invitations to hunt in Ireland. One such friend was Robert Bernard George Ashhurst Gradwell of Dowth Hall in County Meath who had attended the opening ceremony of Fern Library. The Gradwell family had originated in Preston, Lancashire, not far from the original Fletcher home at Woolton Hill in Liverpool, but a later section of the family had settled in County Meath. Robert Gradwell, High Sheriff of County Meath, married Henrietta Maria Plunkett, younger daughter of the 10th Earl of Fingall and it was through these contacts that Fitzroy rented Slane Castle from the Marquis of Conyngham for several hunting seasons.

As a regular participant in the Meath Hunt during the months from November to March, Fitzroy was requiring a more permanent residence in Ireland and, with the help of Richard Gradwell, he found and purchased the estate of Ardmulchan in 1900, not too distant from Slane Castle and in close proximity to Navan, the main town in Meath.

The existing house on the estate was attractive and of Georgian style but was not of sufficient proportions for Fitzroy's requirements. On completion of the purchasing legalities, Fitzroy

69. Fitzroy Fletcher on a hunter considered an excellent mount even in present times. *Courtesy of Private Collection.*

immediately instigated plans to have the house replaced, and having heard of the designing ability of the Edinburgh architect Sydney Mitchell through acquaintances met at Rosehaugh, employed Mitchell's services.

As many of Fitzroy's friends were of titled families or high-ranking Army officers, it was appropriate to have an emblem of importance to complement his position in society and among the hunting fraternity. Fitzroy recorded his Coat-of-Arms in Dublin but not in Scotland.

70. Arms of Fitzroy Fletcher.

The demi-lion holding a crosslet in the right paw and surmounting the quarterly arms is an emblem of deathless courage, and the accompanying armed arm with the sword to the right denotes a man ready for battle. In the shield below, the chevron represents protection and combined with a repeat of the gauntlet from above, would signify readiness to do battle in order to protect - an appropriate sign for a landowner of large estates. The use of the mullets and crescents reinforce the message that the owner has qualities of learning, virtue and piety.

The gauntlet holding a sword is part of the Jack Coat-of-Arms in Scotland but neither Fitzroy nor his brother James Douglas ever registered Arms in Scotland though James Douglas did permit himself the indulgence of having the gauntlet with sword engraved on his specially commissioned array of table crystal, perhaps as a reminder that the family originally bore the name of Jack. "Post Nubila" is the motto associated with the surname of Jack and literally translated means "After the Clouds", or more freely "After the Clouds comes the Sun," but this motto was only used by another branch of the family in England.

A constant companion of Fitzroy was his trusted and beloved Scottish collie "Jock" who faithfully followed his master. It was typical of Fitzroy never to forget such a loyal servant and on the death of Jock, Fitzroy had a stone erected over his grave with the inscription "Jock, a Scotch collie, faithful friend of Fitzroy Fletcher." In addition, Fitzroy had a wood planted behind the stables and named it "Jock's Wood." Throughout his relatively short life, there were many examples of Fitzroy's considerate and caring personality.

71. "Jock" the Scotch collie.
Courtesy of Private Collection.

72. Fitzroy Fletcher with Jock.
Courtesy of Private Collection.

Though a participant in the sport of hunting, Fitzroy was not of a strong constitution having suffered from a heart condition for many years as a result of an attack of rheumatic fever as a child. Although he was full of enthusiasm for his newly planned and costly mansion in Ireland, his health was such that he was forced to delegate many decisions to his trusted and long term manager of Letham Grange, James Stirling, who communicated Fitzroy's wishes and liaised with the architect. By eighteen months, construction had made good progress, but tragically Fitzroy was never to see completion. He died in August 1902 at Letham Grange having suffered a steady deterioration in health during the previous six months. His great attachment to Fern Estate made it appropriate that his remains were laid in Fern Churchyard.

During their short and happy marriage, Fitzroy and Frances Mary were the epitome of the saying "opposites attract". She was an exuberant extrovert and he of a quiet, kindly disposition. Fitzroy revelled in his wife's "joie de vivre" and was ever anxious to please her. The frequently inclement Scottish weather caused her to yearn for the warmer climes of Melbourne to such an extent that Fitzroy had the small conservatory at Letham Grange, which had been erected by his father, replaced with a new very extensive one in which Australian plants such as eucalyptus, mimosa and kumquats were grown. One eucalyptus was so rare that the only other one in the Country was at Kew Gardens. Frances Mary in turn appreciated Fitzroy's gentle tolerance of her ways and held him in very high esteem, as did all who knew him.

Fitzroy's father had trained him well and Fitzroy's Will, drafted by the family solicitors Brodies of Edinburgh, was no less instructive than his father's had been. Apart from the ownership of the lands of Fern, Letham Grange and Ardmulchan, Fitzroy's investments in Britain were largely in railway stock when railways were still in private ownership and each district or area had its own company. Amongst several smaller British holdings were shares in the Bank of England and the Farmers' Mart at Brechin. Railways formed the largest part of his portfolio, even overseas, and there were shares in Indian, Canadian and South American railways. Smaller investments were in the Mersey Docks, the Rosehaugh Tea Company in Ceylon and gold shares in South Africa and Australia. Fitzroy had concerns that the work in progress at Ardmulchan should be completed according to his wishes and his Will allowed for the sum of £7,000 to be used for the decoration and furnishing of the house. With regard to the position of the immediate family, it was stated that should Frances Mary pre-decease Fitzroy, then Conway and Thomas would inherit; otherwise they would inherit on the death of Frances Mary. In the meantime, Conway and Thomas received an annuity and Frances Mary had the life-rent of all the houses, furnishings and income from the estates after expenses. Pre-nuptial contracts were frequently arranged between wealthy families and one had been agreed between Fitzroy and Frances Mary in 1890. His executors would honour this contract, over and above the other bequest. Frances Mary was to receive a list of personal items and the horses, carriages, guns and sporting requisites - a bequest which reflected her keen equestrian interests. Fitzroy's wishes ended on a somewhat poignant and optimistic note that "the Fletcher name be used throughout".

73. The grave of Fitzroy Fletcher.
K. MacLeman.

74. Fitzroy C. Fletcher
of Letham Grange.
Courtesy of Private Collection.

75. Artificial lake with sluice. Letham Grange.

LETHAM GRANGE ESTATE

Having a great interest in agriculture, Fitzroy exhibited prize cattle at annual agricultural shows and also raised a considerable number of thoroughbred horses and Clydesdale stock. His involvement in the Angus Agricultural Association from 1890 to 1896 is recorded in the meticulously documented minutes of the Association. He represented the Arbroath section from 1891 and was Vice-President of the Association in 1892. The Annual Angus Show rotated regularly between Brechin, Forfar and Arbroath and was held on a Saturday early in August; 9th August 1890 at Brechin, 8th August 1891 at Forfar and on the 6th August 1892 at Arbroath.

In the years 1890, 1892 and 1896 Fitzroy was the judge of the class "Other Horses", and therefore could not participate in that class during those years. His successes in 1890 were modest and mainly in poultry and produce but he ventured into the Shorthorn Cattle competitions in 1891, winning three third prizes for which there was no monetary gain, merely a merit credit; however a first prize for 14 lbs. of cured butter was rewarded with 15/-. Traditionally cured butter was made when the cows were taken to higher summer pastures. It was salted fresh butter which was stored in crocks during the summer and then served to the family over the winter when the cows were dry of milk.

Agricultural competitions are no less fiercely fought than any major competitions and after Fitzroy won £1-10/- for the best pony of 12 to 14 hands, Baillie Taylor raised an objection, stating that the pony was over that height. Having had the pony examined and the height verified at less than 14 hands, the Committee declared that the award should stand.

Such objections were a common annual occurrence and in 1892 the Committee agreed that in future a veterinary surgeon would be responsible for all measurements and that thereafter the Committee's decision was to be final.

In that same year, Fitzroy won the prize for the best Guernsey or Jersey cow in the show-yard. His brother James Douglas Fletcher of Rosehaugh was also a great competitor in the agricultural scene but had been able to build successes on the pedigree stock inherited from their father. Whereas Fitzroy was the first of the two brothers to breed Jerseys which were famous for the quality of their milk rather than the quantity, and whereas Fitzroy consistently won a first or second prize for his Shorthorn bulls, James Douglas achieved the greatest success with the Aberdeen Angus heifer "Pride of the Highlands", the formidable British champion of 1893, weighing 17 hundredweight at just under three years.

During the years when he was not acting as judge, Fitzroy won mainly first prizes for his one, two and three year old geldings or fillies. Interestingly, he entered no horses in 1894. In 1896 Fitzroy began to exhibit in the sheep classes and received a first for his Shropshire Down breed. Black Cheviots and Border Leicesters were more successful at Rosehaugh. Fitzroy withdrew from all committees after 1896.

Alongside his agricultural interests, Fitzroy had a relish for mechanical equipment and from 1886 onwards made continuous improvements on the estate. He installed a fully equipped model dairy and had a turbine generator station erected on the premises to provide electricity for the main house and all the buildings within the policies.

Between October 1895 and March 1896, extensive changes were carried out at the home farm where a large new steading was erected with a frontage extending to two hundred feet. Three massive cattle courts with concrete floors were flanked by feeding byres, stables, turnip sheds and loose-boxes fitted with the most modern Musgrave's patent mangers.

76. The stables section of the home farm, Letham Grange 1896.
Courtesy of Private Collection.

The cattle courts were enclosed with iron fencing and fitted with iron troughs. The stables section contained seven stalls floored with Musgrave's blue brick and was connected to hay and straw sheds, boiler house and traction engine house. A threshing mill with a straw elevator of the newest design, a corn room, sheaf loft, granary and cart sheds completed what was now one of the largest and best-equipped steadings in the country. This was in 1896.

77. The stables and coach-house at Letham Grange with traditional clock above centre arch - 1896.
Courtesy of Private Collection.

Fitzroy's own well-appointed stables, occupied by the grooms, horses and carriages, were also considerably extended. The grooms' accommodation in the eastern wing was converted to provide five additional stalls for the horses. An elaborate new ceiling of pitch pine was installed by the estate carpenters and the fitting of the stalls was entrusted to the firm of Messrs. Musgrove & Co. Ltd. of Belfast. This firm also fitted adamantine flooring and cream tiles to the walls. The most modern of equipment had been installed and brightness, comfort and cleanliness pervaded all areas of the stables. The ten grooms employed were now given accommodation in a new spacious two-storey building attached to the existing riding school erected some years previously. The grooms were provided with hot and cold baths, wash-hand basins and "other conveniences".

Even the smithy or blacksmith's shop had been upgraded and was now a model of its kind with the fitting of a steam hammer capable of the force of a two-ton weight and a turbine blower which was propelled by a 4 horse-power engine.

Six farms, along with the new steading at the home farm, were supplied with water from windmill power. Such innovative measures by Fitzroy were not only beneficial to the economic management of the estate but greatly improved the quality of everyday life for his employees and tenants and demonstrated his consideration for their well-being.

Most large houses of that era had walled kitchen gardens of considerable size but Fitzroy proceeded to further enlarge those at Letham Grange by incorporating newly constructed and extensive glass hothouses which were designed and erected by the specialist firm of MacKenzie and Moncur. These hothouses provided the estate owners with a selection of exotic fruits and vegetables which they had first savoured on their trips abroad. The photographs clearly display the complex hot-water piping system which generated heat for the required temperatures for successful cropping and provided the necessary frost protection. The outside growing area was also extended and Fitzroy then had both the

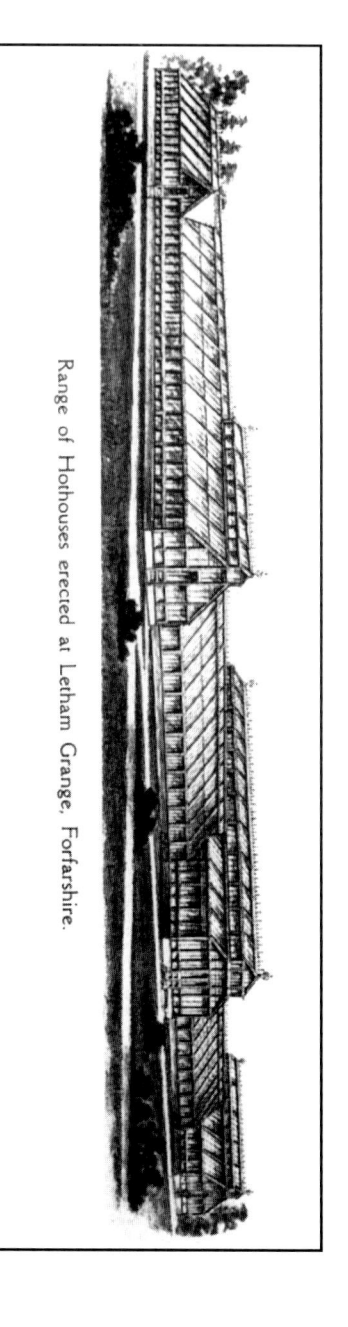

Range of Hothouses erected at Letham Grange, Forfarshire.

MACKENZIE & MONCUR, LIMITED, EDINBURGH, LONDON, AND GLASGOW.

78. *Crown Copyright: R.C.A.H.M.S.*

79. The greenhouses at Letham Grange built by Mackenzie & Moncur.
Courtesy of Private Collection.

80. The greenhouses and walled-garden, Letham Grange.
Courtesy of Private Collection.

81. An abundance of grapes at Letham Grange.
Courtesy of Private Collection.

gardens and policies enclosed by a handsome well-crafted stone wall. Many years later the greenhouses produced tomatoes on a commercial basis.

82. The heating system in the vinery, Letham Grange.
Courtesy of Private Collection.

During the period of 1895 to 1896, further improvements included a virtual reconstruction of the farmhouse and the erection of a two storey cottage of considerable size sited in a park to the east of the vineries as accommodation for the head gardener.

Throughout the years of improvements, Fitzroy relied considerably on James Stirling, the factor of the estate, who, not only attended to daily management but also had the ability to draw plans for buildings and oversee their construction. James Stirling's son, also named James Stirling followed family tradition and held the same post in later years.

Fitzroy's tastes for mechanical pursuits extended to a modicum of self-indulgence in the form of a miniature railway which, complete with locomotive and a carriage to accommodate passengers, moved round the grounds.

83. Fitzroy and Frances Mary Fletcher with the miniature locomotive at Letham Grange. *Courtesy of Private Collection.*

COUNTY MEATH, THE RIVER BOYNE AND ARDMULCHAN.

Even in a country with a history as long and proud as that of Ireland, the history of County Meath is outstanding in antiquity and richness, stretching back to Neolithic times and the earliest settlements of man in Ireland. From the estuary of the river Boyne at Drogheda, early man migrated inland leaving magnificent examples of monumental tombs at New Grange, Dowth and Knowth for later generations to view in awe. The Ireland of pre-Christian times was divided into five kingdoms or provinces and the province of Meath boasted the site of Tara where the all-powerful high kings of Ireland were crowned and resided.

Though history has attributed St. Patrick with the honour of introducing Christianity to the Country, there was knowledge of it in Ireland before his time. When the rest of Europe succumbed to the Dark Ages, Ireland alone remained unaffected and during its Golden Age it was referred to as "The Island of Saints and Scholars". It would be impossible to write of Meath without mention of "the most beautiful illuminated manuscript in the world" - the Book of Kells, hand-written and decorated about the 8th century by the monks at Kells. Richly ornamented in gold and colours, the work is so fine that one hundred and fifty-eight interlacing bands have been counted in one square inch.

It is perhaps less well-known that Admiral Sir Francis Beaufort, who devised the Beaufort Scale for navigational use and who had the Beaufort Sea, north of the Arctic Circle named after him, was born at Navan in 1774. Navan is the main town of Meath and though it was originally a market town, it has since seen the development of mining for its rich lead and zinc deposits.

The position, climate and rich soil of Meath were the factors which encouraged settlement. The County lies to the north-west of Dublin but its equitable temperatures are suitable for producing lush vegetation and rich grasslands - grasslands which have led to the use of the phrase "Meath of the Pastures". Although it is a district for the growing of wheat and flax, an experiment was successfully carried out in 1898 for the growing of tobacco but the onset of the First World War ended any further plans.

With such rich pastures available, it is not surprising that Meath has been, and continues to be, an important area for the breeding and training of racehorses. Irish-bred horses often win the world's greatest races and many champions have been trained at Irish stables with County Meath producing two winners of the Irish Grand National.

Meath produced the pedigree stock of hunters much sought after by the Irish and British gentry for the sport of hunting. The growing popularity of fox-hunting in the early to middle 1800s saw some districts suffer a dearth of foxes for the hunt and deer were introduced as a replacement quarry. Hunting flourished in the area with the season starting in October and continuing to February or March depending on whether it was a hunt for foxes or deer. Gathering unrest in agricultural life in the 1800s brought about changes in attitude and fox-hunting was temporarily halted in particular areas; but the unabating demand for pedigree hunters as cavalry mounts, as well as for home and overseas sport, saw the construction of numerous stud stables. Many stables were built at great expense and with as much attention to detail as to a house; but changing attitudes caused later constructions to be more practical and less ostentatious. The Meath Hunt remains a well-known and respected hunt and is held over the winter months.

84. Preparations for the Hunt at Ardmulchan.
Courtesy of Private Collection.

85. A Stable in Ireland - circa 1900. Location is unknown.
Courtesy of Private Collection.

86. County Meath.

THE RIVER BOYNE.

The Boyne is a river of great beauty, a beauty aptly recorded by Sir William Wilde, father of Oscar Wilde, in his book "The Beauties of the Boyne and the Blackwater".

"Among the many scenes of beauty and of interest with which this fair island abounds, we know of none which combines such variety of the former or so many objects of the latter as the "pleasant Boyne."

With its source in County Kildare, the Boyne meanders a course of seventy miles through Meath to a sea outlet at Drogheda. It was its very existence which encouraged the early settlers to explore and move inland from the sea-shore. On this occasion, interest is not in the unquestionable beauty of the Boyne but in its role as a means of transporting goods between Drogheda and Navan. Ideas were proposed in 1710 for the use of flat-bottomed boats to bring heavy loads of rock, gravel and clay to Navan.

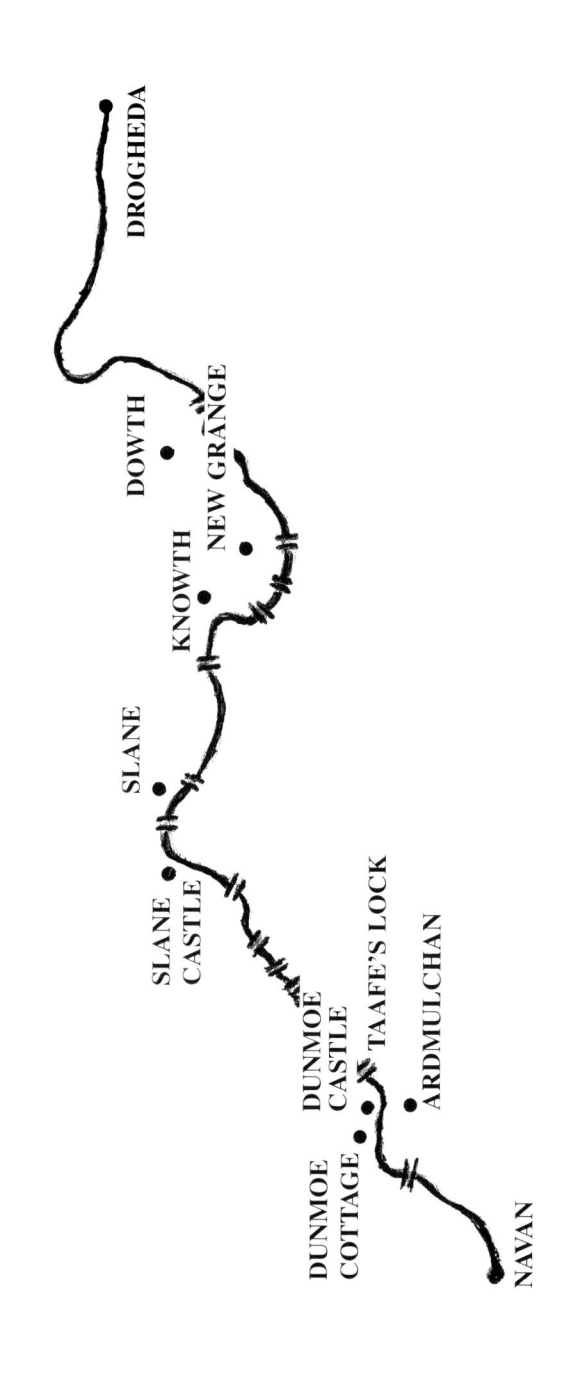

87. Map of the river Boyne from Drogheda to Navan.

The growth of flour and flax mills in the 18th century depended greatly on the harnessing of the waters of the Boyne for power, but increased production created a need for a suitable and cheap method of transport for exporting from the port at Drogheda.

At Drogheda problems existed with the restriction of the navigation channel, while the unpredictable behaviour of the waters of the estuary presented unwary captains with hazards. Most ships in the years prior to the advent of steam carried a burden of less than two hundred tons and this fact is significant when their role is considered in a later chapter. A survey was made of the river and plans were instigated for the construction of a canal between Drogheda and Navan with a later section to continue to Trim. Part of the finance for this project was raised through a series of unusual taxes - a coach and chariot tax, a card and dice tax, a gold and silver tax, and, at a later date, a tax on sporting and hunting dogs - all the necessary luxuries for the gentry.

Work began in 1748 under the supervision of Thomas Steers, the first great British navigation engineer. Eight locks were planned for the section between Drogheda and Slane and the canal progressed satisfactorily to this point, much to the delight of the owners of a massive mill being built at Slane, but this well-constructed stretch had drained much of the finance and it resulted in further work up-stream being of a poorer quality.

During the process of construction, a conflict of interests arose with those who had reaped benefits over many years from the profusion of salmon and trout in the river. The Boyne had a reputation for containing salmon of over thirty pounds and the landowners on both sides of its banks gained financially from the sale of the fish caught or from the leasing of the lucrative fishing rights. The installation of the locks and the construction works in general made it difficult for the salmon to reach up-stream to spawn. This situation would have been equally upsetting to the poachers who saw their livelihood disappear.

Throughout its unpredictable existence, the Boyne Navigation Company was bedevilled with financial problems over and above those presented by the river itself.

88. The river Boyne at Slane.
*Courtesy of National Library of Ireland.
Lawrence Collection NS 8713*

An over-abundance of water in winter and inadequate water levels in summer could restrict the use of the nineteen-mile-long waterway. Considerable skill was required to navigate the changes from the canal to river to canal sections and at the same time to contend with transferring the horse from the towpath on the north-side to the south-side and vice versa.

Stoic determination saw the completion of the canal from Drogheda to Navan in 1800 when boats, capable of carrying a forty to sixty tons burden, were able to navigate it. Unfortunately a transport competitor appeared in the shape of improved roads between Navan and Dublin and it became more economic for the merchants in Navan and Trim to use the roads. The arrival of the railway was a further blow. Loss of revenue and the financial burden of on-going maintenance saw the fortunes of the Navigation Company decline.

The turn of the century saw a temporary revival of the canal as a tourist attraction offering pleasure cruises to savour the beauty of the Boyne; but this limited use could not provide the required income and the Company went into liquidation in 1913. In recent years suggestions have been made that limited areas be revived for tourist use but, as with all rural areas, considerable frequency of use is vital to make it viable.

ARDMULCHAN.

When James Fletcher bought Letham Grange, he bought a portion of the early history of Arbroath; when Fitzroy Fletcher bought Ardmulchan, he bought an important part of the early history of County Meath.

The name Ardmulchan, or Ard Mullachain, has been translated as meaning "The hill of the little summit" or "Mealchu's height," and it is recorded that a battle took place here in 968 with the Norman victor carrying his spoils back to Dublin.

The importance of Ardmulchan arises from its position on the Boyne and from a natural ford which existed there in mediaeval times, crossing to Donaghmore on the north bank where there had been a church. A smaller church stood on the south bank and a well was situated in the Ardmulchan grounds close to the ford; this all suggested a route well used by the travellers of that time. As a townland or estate, it was always accorded strategic importance, an importance reflected in the military or governmental men of substance who were granted the lands from the Crown. The remains of the very substantial Castle Dunmoe stand guard close to this point on the Boyne, again suggesting the strategic value of the site.

89. The remains of Dunmoe Castle.
K. MacLeman.

In the Civil Survey of 1654, the lands of Ardmulchan are stated as having, "a castle, a church, a tuck-mill and several cottages." Ardmulkin Parish was a portion of the Barony of Skreen which was a district of "great tillage and grazing with no bog". At the time of an Ordinance Survey carried out in 1836, the Earl of Mayo owned much of the Parish of Ardmulkin except the townland of Ardmulchan, which, in this survey, stretched to approximately one thousand, one hundred and fifty-six acres including twenty-five acres of the River Boyne. The River Boyne and canal form the north boundary to the lands and the road between Navan and Drogheda borders the south side. At a point below Ardmulchan, the Boyne sweeps in a curve into a broad bay where the valley widens- an area prone to flooding. Above and below this point, locks were constructed on the canal. Each of the twenty canal locks was named either after its location, as in Slane Castle Lock, or after the owner of the adjoining land. The landowners were usually shareholders of the Navigation Company and the lock below Ardmulchan was known as Taafe's Lock after Robert Taafe, the owner of these lands.

The Taafe Family, also spelt Taaffe, acquired the Ardmulchan Estate during the late 1800s and has been credited with the building of a house and offices, the laying-out of a garden and the planting of trees on the grounds. They remained owners until it was sold to Fitzroy Fletcher in 1900, and though the Wyndham Land Act of 1903 caused more of the larger estates to be sold and divided into farming units, the Ardmulchan Estate remained relatively unaffected.

90. The banks of the Boyne and Dunmoe ruins

91. Mr. A. G. S. Mitchell.
Crown Copyright: RCAHMS.

ARTHUR GEORGE SYDNEY MITCHELL.

Sydney Mitchell was a most resourceful and prolific architect in Edinburgh during the late 19th and early 20th centuries. He was born in 1856 at Headswood Cottage, Larbert, in Stirlingshire of parents who came from very different backgrounds. His mother, Margaret Hay Houston, came originally from Cromdale in the Highlands and was of a wealthy agricultural family. George Mitchell, grandfather of Sydney, was a civil engineer and Arthur his father, was born at Lane End in Staffordshire. At the time of the marriage in 1855 at Headswood Cottage, Arthur was twenty-eight years, a qualified doctor of medicine and resident in Glasgow. After Sydney's birth, the family moved to Edinburgh where his father took up the position of Departmental Commissioner for the Act of Lunacy for Scotland, a position which was to enable his son to set out on his career with considerable privilege.

Having been educated privately and then at Edinburgh University, Sydney was fortunate in being trained in the offices of Sir Rowand Anderson, an architect of great renown. Five years later and at the age of twenty-six, Sydney commenced his own practice in 1882, initially from the family home at 34 Drummond Place. He immediately received major commissions through the business and social connections of his father who was also now a Fellow of the Society of Antiquaries of Scotland and, with the assurance of such commissions, Sydney transferred his centre of operations to 122 George Street.

To receive a commission with no restrictions on expenditure must be the dream of any architect at any stage of his career; to receive such a commission at the outset of one's career must have made Sydney the envy of many.

Number three, Rothesay Terrace, Edinburgh, owned by John Ritchie Finlay, the proprietor of the "Scotsman", was that assignment. John Finlay was a very influential personage in Edinburgh and those of literary fame such as William Makepeace Thackery and Thomas Carlisle frequented his home. Through the influence of his daily publications, Finlay advocated the admitting of women to the Edinburgh Medical School and through his benevolence had major improvements made in 1883 to the living conditions of the people in the Well Court, an area which could be viewed from the rear of his home at Rothesay Terrace and which formed part of the Dean Village.

Sydney Mitchell began the transformation of Number Three, Rothesay Terrace from the point of entry. The house originally formed part of a continuous style of street architecture and though the exterior dimensions remained unaltered, Sydney transfigured the façade by designing a carved wooden porch and canopy to protrude from the entrance, thus making the house immediately distinctive from the remainder of the street. Wrought iron railings were added to the windows of the second floor and to a central first floor window, the function of which was changed to form an opening to a balcony.

As a building of seven levels, it has five facing towards the street and two "semi-basement" levels at the rear which, at that time, contained the 'downstairs" area and the traditional access for the servants and goods.

For many, the point of interest on entering a house is the staircase. The stairwell at Rothesay Terrace dominates the heavily panelled hall with light radiating from a lofty concave roof-light and echoing from the bright plaster of the walls. Three arches span the width of the hall with two pillars of these interrupting the flow of the left-hand banister of the stair. The wrought iron balustrade and the arches provide a revealing view of the direction of the stair. Light, green-veined marble treads add to an overall contrast with the profusion of wood in the foyer.

93. The Porch of No. 3 Rothesay Terrace.
K. MacLeman.

92. Rothesay Terrace.
K. MacLeman.

94. The Stairwell.
K. MacLeman.

95. The Griffins and Newels.
K. MacLeman.

Each heavily-carved newel of the right-hand banister is mounted with a crouched griffin. The plasterwork of the ceiling above the stairwell carries a frieze of swags and foliage and the decoration continues into the window recess and to the edge of the glass panels.

Through the main arch of the hall there is access to the banqueting room. With the house having a north exposure, the preponderance of wood on the ceiling tends to make the room dark but daylight illuminates the three, yellow and green, personalised window panels and reflects on the rich opulence of the frieze which contains golden cherubs carrying swags of fruit on a green background, all bordered by wooden rails. The most imposing of fireplaces maintains the prosperous theme. The overmantel rises to the ceiling and the complete chimney-piece has been intricately carved.

96. The Frieze of the Banqueting Room.
K. MacLeman.

97. One of the three personalised windows.
K. MacLeman.

98. The overmantel of the fireplace in the Banqueting Room.
K. MacLeman.

99. The fireplace of the Banqueting Room.
K. MacLeman.

In contrast to this room, the drawing room, situated immediately above, has a brighter appearance. The marble fireplace, which has inserts of green rectangles and terra cotta circles, is a focal point on entry but the oak ceiling has to be the most remarkable feature. It has been inserted the length of the room with ornamented rectangles of gilt and green, and around these, on all sides, are further gilt-edged, painted panels depicting scenes from Greek Mythology with each panel bearing a centre medallion representing wisdom, gentleness and other admirable traits. A white plaster frieze of cherubs and trailing foliage lightens the richness of the gold, green and oak ceiling.

The central window gives access to a balcony overlooking the Dean Village and viewing from this extension on the fourth floor at the rear, can produce a feeling of vertigo, due to the severe drop of the ground elevation.

100. The marble fireplace of the Drawing Room.
K. MacLeman.

101. One of the centre ceiling panels in the Drawing Room.
K. MacLeman.

102. One of the side ceiling panels in the Drawing Room.
K. MacLeman.

There are many points of detail to be observed throughout the house - ornate brass escutcheons, beautifully shaped brass hinges, fine beading to the panelling. The library, which is lined in cedar, has a "minstrels" gallery supported all round by an arching of the wood panelling. The marble fireplace has added tiled panels representing the arts of music and painting.

103. The marble fireplace in the Library.
K. MacLeman.

The overall impression of the interior of Number Three, Rothesay Terrace, is one of rich opulence and a style very much according to Victorian taste. There has been great attention to the smallest of details and the contrast of light and dark has been used to great effect. As well as there being no limit to the cost, Sydney Mitchell must also have had access to the very best of craftsmen. The works were completed in 1885.

104. The brass escutcheons in the Drawing Room.
K. MacLeman.

105. The "Minstrels" gallery in the Library, Rothesay Terrace.
K. MacLeman.

The increasing volume of work compelled Sydney to employ another architect George Wilson, who was first employed by David Bryce in George Street, Edinburgh and then by Sir Rowand Anderson, a previous partner of Bryce. In 1886, Sydney Mitchell transferred his premises to 13 Young Street, though Wilson continued to work at the George Street office for a time. The combination of Mitchell and Wilson proved to be such a successful one that George Wilson became a partner the following year and the partnership continued to flourish. Wilson made a considerable contribution but his ability as an architect was frequently overshadowed by that of his high profile partner Sydney.

Many are the buildings in the City of Edinburgh which are testimony to the gifted designs of Sydney Mitchell. His productive list of buildings include churches, banks, hospitals, the Edinburgh University Union, the Rainy Hall at the New College, the Jubilee Pavilion at the Royal Infirmary and a most imposing new construction for the Royal Asylum at Craig House, built to accommodate the wealthy mentally ill.

The New Craig House building is also known as the Thomas Clouston Chateau in recognition of the brilliant psychiatrist who did so much towards psychiatry being accepted as a medical science. With the welfare of his patients ever uppermost in his mind, Dr. Clouston travelled widely in search of a new and more humane approach to the treatment of the mentally ill. From these travels was born the idea of providing more relaxed and homely surroundings for the patients. According to reports, the original plans for New Craig House were drawn by an in-patient, formerly a draughtsman, under the direction of Dr. Clouston, and later interpreted and transposed by Sydney Mitchell in 1889 to the style of a French Chateau which contained "an informality of architecture set in opposition to an arched hall with colossal accumulation." This central construction served four out-lying residential villas. The buildings are now under the ownership of Napier University and the main hall provides an illustrious venue for social functions.

106. The central building of New Craig House.
K. MacLeman.

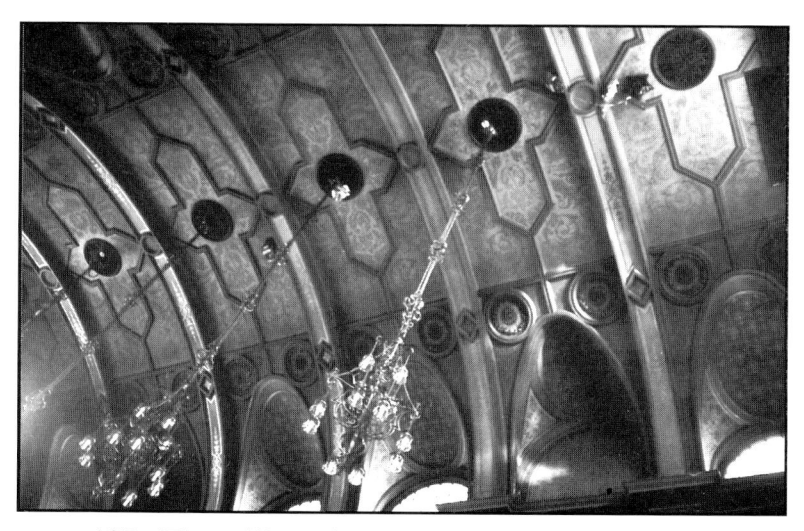

107. The ceiling of the Hall at New Craig House.
K. MacLeman.

108. The ceiling and west window of hall.
K. MacLeman.

109. A part of the east section of the hall.
K. MacLeman.

Apart from this impressive list of commissions, Sydney's business and social connections make for no less impressive reading. Now also a Fellow of the Society of Antiquaries of Scotland, he was architect to the General Board of Lunacy for Scotland, to the Managers of the Royal Infirmary, to the Directors of the Commercial Bank of Scotland, to the Managers of the Royal Asylum, to the Society of Writers to His Majesty's Signet and to the Directors of the Scottish Life Assurance Company - to name but a few. Work was also executed at many of the major country homes including those of the Marquess of Tweeddale, the Earl of Rosebery, the Earl of Home, Lord Haddo and Sir J. Ramsay Maitland, Bart. all of whom visited Rosehaugh Estate in the North of Scotland owned by James Douglas Fletcher, brother of Fitzroy. Their satisfaction with the work of Sydney Mitchell was doubtless related to Fitzroy on such visits when they heard of his plans to construct a mansion in Ireland.

Having viewed some of the buildings designed by Sydney Mitchell, the curious may well have an interest in the style of house that such an architect would build for himself. Sydney had chosen a secluded position surrounded by trees and fields, yet with an open view across a golf course. In 1898 he was the owner of a house, offices, garden and stables at Gullane, east of Edinburgh, but it is not until 1900 that the house was named "the Pleasance". He also owned two other houses in the vicinity, one of which was occupied by his butler and the other, by his gardener.

On completion, the house was photographed by Bedford Lemere and Company, architectural photographers of domestic interiors. From these photographs of 1900, there appears to be no preponderance of wood, no heavy gilding or ornamentation but bright spacious rooms with a profusion of white plasterwork. There is a continuous flow of the rooms from the drawing room through the hallway to the dining room and his predilection for arches has remained, though there is a suggestion of the Arts and Crafts movement in the frieze surrounding the hall.

110. The Morning Room at the Pleasance - 1900.
Crown Copyright : RCAHMS.

111. The Hallway at the Pleasance - 1900.
Crown Copyright : RCAHMS.

The Pleasance was described in 1978 by Colin McWilliam as, "an intimate house, harled and tilehung, behind a single-storey cottage range and having a pretty gatehouse". By 1978 many changes had taken place. Alterations had been made to the building by subsequent owners and its position no longer afforded it the same isolation as in 1900.

Sydney's parents continued to live at 34 Drummond Place and though Sydney had moved to the Pleasance at Gullane, he never married. His mother's death in 1904 was followed in 1909 by that of his father who had earlier been honoured for his many years of service with the title of Sir Arthur Mitchell, KCB. Sydney continued to work for several more years but suffered increasingly from chronic rheumatism and a heart condition. His final commission before retiring was that of the United Free Church headquarters in George Street, Edinburgh in 1911. He died at his home in Gullane in 1930 aged seventy-four years.

112. The Drawing Room at the Pleasance - 1900.
Crown Copyright : RCAHMS.

The Ardmulchan House of the Taafe Family.
Courtesy of Private Collection.

ARDMULCHAN CASTLE.

The Ardmulchan house of 1900, which had served the Taafe Family for many years, was of an attractive Georgian style set amidst a well-established garden. Charming though it was, its dimensions were insufficiently ample and its appearance insufficiently majestic for Fitzroy and Frances Mary Fletcher and the house suffered the great indignity of being replaced.

Fitzroy Fletcher had rented Slane Castle over several hunting seasons from the Marquis of Conyngham. It was an immensely impressive building with battlemented parapets and square turrets and perhaps generated Fitzroy and Frances Mary's concept of a "shooting lodge on the grand scale."

114. Slane Castle.
K. MacLeman.

Dowth Hall, where Fitzroy's friend Robert Gradwell lived, was only a few miles from Slane Castle, and being now well-acquainted with members of the Meath Hunt, Fitzroy hoped to acquire property within the area. Enquiries were made through these friendships and Fitzroy purchased the Ardmulchan Estate from the Taaffe Family about 1899 or early 1900.

An approach was made to the firm of A.G. Sydney Mitchell and Wilson in Edinburgh, the fashionable architects of Scotland at that time who were renowned for transposing an eclectic Renaissance style to private residences. Sydney Mitchell was to design a "shooting lodge" appropriate to Fitzroy's wealthy status.

In a short space of time an acceptable plan had been prepared, and by the autumn of 1900 construction had begun. The original plans do not appear to have survived the passage of time: it is thought that Sydney Mitchell may have surrendered them to his client, as he occasionally did, but to date they have failed to reappear.

Several features incorporated at Ardmulchan had previously been applied at Letham Grange and at Rosehaugh, the home of Fitzroy's brother. Rosehaugh, designed by William Flockhart, was virtually completed by 1900 and Fitzroy had the opportunity on his visits there to observe and take note.

The Boyne area contained large deposits of clay and the rich red glow of these local bricks were used extensively in the new construction. It is regretted that black and white photographs cannot interpret the mellow yet intense colouring of the brick walls. Contrary to the tradition of utilising local materials wherever possible, the stone for the decorative features of Ardmulchan was to be quarried in Scotland, its colour to contrast with that of the red brick. A suitable supply of local limestone, which was hard, enduring and capable of being carved in fine detail, existed at Ardbraccan and the decision to transport stone from Scotland must be disputed.

The Scottish stone was quarried on the Letham Grange Estate and James Stirling, the factor of Letham Grange, was in control of the operation. Considering that quarrying began during the winter months of 1900 to 1901 and continued through to February of 1902, it was no mean task to keep up with the supply required at Ardmulchan. This fact is borne out in a letter sent to Fitzroy from Sydney Mitchell in June of 1901 after a visit he made to Ardmulchan. Mitchell states that work had been held up for the want of stone lintels. He also suggested that Stirling make occasional visits to Navan to inspect the site, in spite of there being a clerk of works, and added that he was relying on Stirling to communicate Fitzroy's wishes. The letter ended on a lighter note commenting on the "charm" of the garden which was full of roses and interesting shrubs. James Stirling was obviously important to the whole operation, a responsibility over and above his commitment as factor of the Letham Grange Estate.

The transporting of the stones was quite a manoeuvre in itself. Having been dressed at Letham, they were taken to Arbroath harbour and loaded on to sailing boats. Steamships were gradually replacing sail but were not used for the journeys to Drogheda, the nearest port to Ardmulchan. Between January 1901 and February 1902, seven boatloads of stones sailed to Drogheda. The first to sail was the "Badger" carrying a cargo of one hundred tons. The "Rachel" followed, leaving Arbroath on the 26th of March and arriving in Drogheda on the 7th of April 1901. In May and August of 1901, the "Walrus" and the "Beaver" carried almost two hundred tons between them. The "Barraconda" and the "Porpoise" both sailed in October and carried a total burden of one hundred and eighty-eight tons. The final trip was that of the "Walrus" which left Arbroath on the 10th of February in 1902 with seventy-one tons of stones and five fathoms of lathwood which had been imported from Riga in Latvia. Wood had been transported along with the stones at other times but was not always recorded. A total of six hundred and forty-nine and a half tons of dressed stone for decoration had been transported by sailing boats on journeys which took from five to

115. The letter from Sydney Mitchell to Fitzroy Fletcher.
Courtesy of Private Collection.

116. The port of Drogheda - circa 1900.
*Courtesy of The National Library of Ireland.
Lawrence collection - IMP 3826.*

Arbroath Harbour Records - 1901.

EXPORTS.

Date	SHIP'S NAME	Where to.	Sail Cloth.	Yarns. Cwts.	Wheat. Qrs.	Barley. Qrs.	Oats. Qrs.	Peas and Beans.	Potatoes. Tons.
1901		Brought Forward			167	1530	165		254
May 10	"Radiant"	Sunderland							68
"	"Footati" ss	Leith				103	335		
14	End of Seventh Month				167	1633	500		322
16	"Inergy"	Shields							89
17	"Maggie" ss	Dundee				400½			
22	"Footati" ss	Leith					47	247	
31	"Nairns" ss	Borghead							
June 3	"Pioneer"	Shields							75
10	"Dart"	Sunderland				160½			

EXPORTS.

Pavement. Tons.	Burnt Ore.	Herring. Barrels.	Sundries, Tons	Potatoes.			Grain.			Miscellaneous.		TOTAL.		
			118	4	4	8	11	19	9	9	10	16	14	3
				1	2	8						1	2	8
							2	18	7			2	18	7
			118¾	5	7	4	14	18	4	9	10	20	15	6
				1	9	8						1	9	8
							3	6	9			3	6	9
							1	16	10			1	16	10
			Stone 100							16	8	16	8	
				1	5	·						1	5	·
							1	6	9			1	6	9
			218¾	8	2	·	21	8	8	1	6	6	30	17	2
				4	12	7						4	12	7

117. *Kind permission of Angus Council Cultural Services.*

thirteen days to complete - the weather and the time of year being important factors. The route taken by the boats is not recorded and it was presumably the decision of the captain whether to sail by the Pentland Firth or the English Channel.

Once the stone had reached Drogheda it was transferred to "lighters" for the last stage up the river Boyne. Having negotiated the numerous locks of the Boyne Canal and having passed through Taafe's lock just below Ardmulchan, the "lighters" would have tied up at a point before the weir at Dunmoe. (See map on p.117) This location was at the riverside below the house site. It had been a long journey from the quarries of Letham Grange but it is to be wondered if any, or how many, of these stones fell to the bottom of the Boyne on the last stage.

Though Ardmulchan is still in existence, it remains a private home. The following descriptions relate to the house as it was in the early 1900s and do not take into account any changes of the different uses of rooms or any alterations carried out by owners since 1956.

Both the site and his client presented Sydney Mitchell with a dilemma. It was impossible to provide the public rooms with the maximum of warmth and light from the sun while also having the magnificent view of the river. Be it Fitzroy or be it Mitchell who made the final decision, the river triumphed and the public rooms faced north and to the Boyne.

Mitchell's design of the front porch may have been over ornate for some tastes. Tuscan pillars, paired on either side of the opening were surmounted by a Doric frieze, which in turn was surmounted by pediments, all of which was mounted by two heraldic and savage looking lions. It contrasted heavily with the fragility of the mullioned windows on either side. Extensions three storeys high were added to the west and east of this central section. Built in warm red brick, they rose majestically, plain and unadulterated with the only concession to adornment being the use of the imported limestone around the windows.

118. The front entrance of Ardmulchan.
K. MacLeman.

119. Ardmulchan on completion.
Courtesy of Private Collection.

On the side facing the Boyne, three bays were constructed to a height of three storeys and were connected by narrow gabled sections. At the north-west end, an embattled tower with arcaded windows soared above the remainder of the house, giving yet another vantage-point from where to view the countryside. Fitzroy had obviously not been deterred by the "ups and downs" of the tower at Letham Grange. This tower served a dual purpose: its southwest pier had been enlarged to house the water tanks necessary for a continual supply of piped hot and cold water.

120. The three bays with the connecting sections.
K. MacLeman.

When involved in a large commission, architects preferred, where possible, to work with tradesmen and craftsmen whom they knew. Distance and other business commitments meant that Sydney Mitchell could only visit Ardmulchan occasionally and therefore he had to rely on the men at Ardmulchan who had worked with him previously and would have some idea of what he required at certain stages of construction.

121. The southwest pier which housed the water tanks.
K. MacLeman.

The Glasgow and Dublin firm of G. Rome and Company had carried out the decorative plasterwork at Letham Grange for James Fletcher and with a branch at Dublin, they were an obvious choice to carry out the high standard of work required at Ardmulchan. All of the ground floor rooms exhibited their decorative plasterwork, lightening the effect of the oak panelling. The skill of the craftsmen at Ardmulchan had the same superior quality as it had at Letham Grange.

In the interior of the house, the hall was a pivotal area from where the other public rooms radiated and in spite of it being extensively panelled there was an impression of great illumination. Daylight radiated through the liberal amount of glass inserted in the wall to the right of the front doorway. This mullioned window was reminiscent of a similar window at Rosehaugh which lit the otherwise gloomy main stair. The hall at Ardmulchan gained further light from a second though smaller mullioned window to the left of the entrance and the upper lights of these windows contained leaded glass motifs of a heraldic nature.

With due awareness of the fact that Ardmulchan was a shooting lodge rather than a town house, Sydney exhibited self-restraint when designing the oak panelling of the hall and the staircase. There were no heraldic griffins on the newels as there had been at Rothesay Terrace and the whole effect was very much less pretentious with rounded sandstone replacing the wood pillars for the arch support. A minstrel's gallery overlooked the hall but being much reduced in size compared to the one at Rothesay Terrace, it was decorative rather than practical.

The customary public rooms - the drawing room, dining room, boudoir or morning room, study or business room - were all accounted for, including, of course, the room without which no mansion was considered complete - the billiard room. The panelling of the billiard room duplicated that of the hall and the gentlemen were able to relax here, seated in the inglenook by the fireplace while being observed from the corner by a stuffed capercaillie.

122. The mullioned window with heraldic motifs.
K. MacLeman.

    In addition to the white plasterwork of the ceiling, the drawing room had white wall panels inset with red and white tapestry squares. The parquet flooring and the seating arrangement round the room were particularly suitable for the period when it was used for children's parties and dancing classes.

The boudoir, on the other hand, was considered to be a cold room and an attempt was made to make it more habitable with the addition of rush matting which was spread below the Persian carpets.

The fireplace of the dining room was where there was the strongest echo of Rosehaugh. Dining at Rosehaugh had been referred to as "like eating in an Italian Renaissance chapel," and though there was no similarity in the décor of the two dining rooms, the fireplace of Ardmulchan could have compared favourably with the white Italian marble fireplace of Rosehaugh. Just outside the dining room door was a hand operated telephone which was connected directly to the stable-yard, particularly convenient at the times of the hunt to check that one's mount was saddled and ready.

123. The Dining Room fireplace at Rosehaugh.
Thomas Love & Sons, Perth.

124. The Dining Room fireplace at Ardmulchan.
Courtesy of Private Collection.

In his provision of ultimate comfort for his guests, Fitzroy had Sydney Mitchell design large bedrooms with dressing rooms attached and three had "ensuite" facilities. One bedroom may have lacked the view of the Boyne but it had the compensation of an adjacent bathroom and dressing room. The two principal rooms not only had dressing rooms and bathrooms but had baths with the addition of showers in the form of jets of water spraying from holes in the surround at the end. Similar baths had been installed at Rosehaugh but one wonders what James Fletcher would have thought of these innovative ideas.

125. One of the marble baths of Rosehaugh
with the controls on the right-hand side.
D. MacLeman.
Courtesy of Avoch Heritage Association.

A viewing window had been placed in the wall of the corridor leading to the bedrooms, giving sight of the hall below. As this passage continued to its final bend, it widened into an arched balcony of oak which overlooked the hall and was of a length equal to the width of the hall. A position on this balcony permitted close inspection of the plaster ceiling and the craftwork of G. Rome and Company.

The rooms of the top floor were built into the roof space with coomb-ceilings and coal fires. Without the benefit of roof insulation, the lasting memory of them was the icy cold temperatures - an atmosphere which would have then been considered character building! Two rooms were used in later years as a nursery and playroom - conveniently placed for the nanny and sufficiently distant for the disrupting noises of "Cowboys and Indians" not to be heard by the guests. Apart from one or two, these rooms were rarely used as many of the servants lived in cottages on the estate.

Complying with convention, access for the servants and supplies was through a small courtyard where there was also a range of ancillary outhouses. The heating boilers were installed in one of these outhouses and a massive one, which supplied the heat for the pipes in the main rooms, must have been similar to the boilers at Letham Grange and Rosehaugh as it had a similarly voracious appetite for fuel. A lesser boiler provided hot water.

The rooms in the basement branched off from a long corridor and included the customary cellars, pantry, servants' hall and kitchen. The kitchen was well equipped for its period and was tiled and well ventilated. As it was on a lower level from the dining room, a pulley-operated "dumb waiter" was installed and food was raised to a pantry immediately off the dining room: an arrangement much appreciated by both the diners, who now received meals at warmer temperatures, and the servants, who no longer had to hasten up stairs carrying meals, always open to the risk of being accidentally dropped.

Whereas Letham Grange appeared to have no laundry and Rosehaugh had a grandiose one designed by William Flockhart, Ardmulchan had one of a moderate size close by the kitchen. It was furnished with numerous tubs, wringers, boiler and drying pulleys but it gradually fell into disuse as the years went by.

Fitzroy had an artificial lake constructed at Letham Grange in 1890s, the water of which was used to turn the turbines for the provision of electricity to the house and the surrounding buildings. A similar arrangement was made at Ardmulchan. In his book "Yellow Furze Memories", Conor Brennan relates how the system worked. *"A pond and power house was built and a turbine charged fifty eight storage batteries. In later years an oil engine was installed as back up for the times when there was a water shortage. Water was pumped to the tanks in the tower and these supplied the house, stables, yard and farmyard. Cables were run underground to the house and yard. When this system was replaced in the 1950s, the wiring and fittings were still in good order."*

126. The Power House.
K. MacLeman.

The River Boyne had always been an important aspect in the design of Ardmulchan. Gardens had existed in the time of the Taafe family and a grassy embankment swept from the site to the edges of the river. Mitchell's reference in 1901 to the colourful bushes and roses of the gardens would suggest that this area had always been utilised and maintained for the family's pleasure. The suggestion of terracing was divided by an elongated flight of steps which ended at a sheltered and secluded plateau by the riverside.

127. The Garden Steps sweeping to the riverbank.
K. MacLeman.

Dunmoe Cottage was situated on the other bank, almost directly opposite, and it may have been while crossing between the two banks at this point that the story, referred to in Conor Brennan's book, occurred. In later years, when Thomas Fletcher was owner of the estate, Billy Ogle was employed there. While crossing the river in the course of his work, Billy accidentally dropped a cross-cut saw in the water. Irritated by this loss, Thomas spoke sharply to Billy - *"Ogle, you lost the saw."* The situation was brilliantly deflated with Billy's reply, *"Nothing is lost when you know where it is."* Perhaps it was this innate sense of humour and the ability to reduce the seemingly "important" to an unimportant level which endeared the area to Fitzroy, Frances Mary and Thomas Fletcher.

When James Fletcher died in October 1885, he had been denied the pleasure of inspecting the fulfilment of his plans for Letham Grange. His son Fitzroy was likewise denied the pleasure of seeing and living in Ardmulchan. Though the house had almost reached completion at the time of his death in August 1902, the furnishings still had to be attended to. His family however continued to enjoy Ardmulchan and its surroundings until the year 1956.

128. Frances Mary on the left, with her mother and Thomas at the door of a recently completed Ardmulchan.
Courtesy of Private Collection.

129. Ardmulchan, County Meath.
Courtesy of Private Collection.

130. Frances Mary Grant later Fletcher.
Courtesy of Private Collection.

FRANCES MARY GRANT, CONWAY AND THOMAS.

Frances Mary, the second daughter of James MacPherson Grant, was born in Melbourne in 1858 and married at the age of nineteen to Francis Sidney Stephen, a solicitor in Melbourne and grandson of Sidney Stephen, Supreme Judge of New Zealand. They had three children but the marriage did not survive long after the birth of the youngest, Thomas, in 1882. Frances Mary's strong personality and beauty was admired by Fitzroy on their first meeting in Australia, and after their marriage in London in 1890, Frances Mary settled at Letham Grange in Scotland. Only her two sons, Conway and Thomas had travelled with her. Her daughter Claudia remained in Australia but on several occasions did journey to visit at Letham Grange.

Frances Mary quickly adapted to the position of wealthy landowner's wife and soon indulged her love of horses and riding, an interest already much enjoyed by her husband Fitzroy. So that Conway and Thomas could be taught to ride both safely and competently, Fitzroy had an indoor riding school built at Letham Grange for that purpose. Years later the riding premises, with the addition of a wooden floor, became a badminton and tennis court.

Social etiquette in Scotland as in England existed by a code of rules which Frances Mary found stifling. The more relaxed atmosphere of society in Ireland was therefore an added pleasure for her along with the great facilities for hunting. Fitzroy's death created a great void in her life and she found it difficult to mingle in society as an unaccompanied widow. She was not present at the marriage of Fitzroy's niece Violet Mary Hope to Brodie of Brodie at Rosehaugh in April 1904.

On the completion and furnishing of Ardmulchan House, she spent more and more time in County Meath. The management of the estates was the responsibility of factors appointed by Fitzroy's Trustees and it was not necessary for Frances Mary to visit Letham Grange too often, though she did return for the grouse-shooting season. At Ardmulchan a young man, Redmond Walter MacGrath, second son of William MacGrath of Toonagh in County Clare, had been given the position of factor and Frances Mary found his company amusing. The friendship developed and much to the consternation of others, a marriage took place in 1905 in Dublin when Frances Mary was forty-seven years and Redmond MacGrath was twenty-seven. The obstacles of social disapproval, the gap in ages and the later intervention of the First World War all proved too great and the marriage began to founder.

Frances Mary's sister Isabel Elizabeth (Dot), widow of John Ferrier Hamilton and their mother, Mary MacPherson Grant, had both moved from Australia to live at Letham Grange. John Ferrier Hamilton's sister Georgina Jane had married Alfred Nevett Fletcher, Fitzroy's eldest brother. Sadly Isabel Elizabeth died in 1912 but Mary Grant, though of advanced years, was still able to sit in the gardens of Letham Grange and enjoy the company of her grandson Thomas and her great-grandchildren on one of their visits from Ireland. She had reached the great age of eighty seven years when she died in 1922.

During the years of the First World War, Ardmulchan House was closed and Frances Mary resided at Letham Grange where facilities were provided for convalescent servicemen, many of whom were Australian. The Republic of Ireland, though not directly involved in the First World War, did provide large numbers of voluntary servicemen. Redmond MacGrath acted as a temporary commander of the Royal Navy Voluntary Reserve and for services rendered received an O.B.E.

131. The riding school building at Letham Grange.
K. MacLeman.

132. Mary Grant with her grandson Thomas in the walled-garden at Letham Grange.
Courtesy of Private Collection.

Unionist Garden Party at Letham Grange 1919.

133. Seated from the left:- Mrs Shaw; Mrs F. C. Fletcher, Letham Grange; Mrs Carnegie, Kirriemuir; Miss Nicol Reedie.

Towards the end of September in the same year as her divorce from Redmond MacGrath, 1919, Frances Mary hosted a garden party for the Colliston and St Vigeans Unionist Association, when the newly appointed Member of Parliament, Captain Shaw, met his constituents for the first time. The weather remained fine though cold and the visitors sauntered round the grounds and gardens while enjoying the games and competitions provided. The Arbroath Pipe Band played while the pupils of the Misses Scott gave dancing performances dressed in Irish costume.

At such gatherings it was usual for descriptions of the ladies' outfits to be reported in the local press and your standing in local society designated your position on the list - if in fact you were mentioned at all. Skunk fur collars and wraps, black silk or straw hats and ostrich feathers were the vogue of the time.

Mrs Fletcher wore a white silk jersey coat over a mist-grey georgette dress with a tunic fringed at the hem and a toque of blue velvet with a floating veil of black lace. A handsome white fox-fur scarf completed her outfit. Lady Baxter was dressed in a smartly tailored ivory white serge coat and skirt with the accessories of a skunk wrap, black hat and ostrich feathers. Amongst the ladies present were Mrs Fagan, Miss Holmes, Mrs F F MacDonald of Cliff House, Arbroath and Miss Moir of St Andrews who wore a purple suit faced with a black and white ostrich feather ruffle and a hat of black and gold "broche" silk. Miss Edith Grant of Woodside's outfit was also worthy of mention - a tete-de-negre gaberdine costume with a beige silk collar, a shoulder strap of skunk and a black silk hat with a long drooping black plume.

Frances Mary's elder son Conway had married Ruby Gordon Wilmer, younger daughter of Colonel John Randal Wilmer, R.A. in 1910, the young couple having met while playing golf at St. Andrews. Of Frances' two sons, Conway was much the more serious and was of great intellect, studying at St. Andrews University and becoming prolific in his knowledge of languages: he was fluent in six, including Japanese. Not only was he an ardent athlete, horseman, swimmer and golfer but he was also proficient as a violinist.

Along with his brother Thomas he had travelled extensively, visiting Japan and Egypt. They had lengthy visits to Ceylon where James Douglas Fletcher, their uncle, had tea plantations. They also journeyed west to Canada where they made hunting expeditions, bringing home the fashionable trophies of those times. After their marriage, Conway and Ruby lived on Vancouver Island in Canada for a short time before returning to Letham Grange to manage the estate.

134. Upper photograph - Conway Fletcher in Ceylon 1911.
Courtesy of Private Collection.
135. Lower photograph - Thomas Fletcher in Egypt 1911.
Courtesy of Private Collection.

136. Conway Fletcher (left) and Thomas Fletcher (middle) at Dambrilla, Ceylon - 1911.
Courtesy of Private Collection.

137. Conway Fletcher - standing beside a Talbot car. Hapugah, Ceylon - 1911.
Courtesy of Private Collection.

Now divorced and aged 61 years, Frances Mary was a lonely figure but still of a strong disposition. She had a great dislike of the term "Grandmama" and insisted that her grandchildren refer to her as "Madam".

138. Frances Mary Fletcher, "Madam"
at Letham Grange House - 1920.
Courtesy of Private Collection.

She withdrew increasingly from local social occasions but continued with her annual trip to France, staying first in Paris in the vicinity of the Boulevard des Capucines and then at the Hotel Carlton in Cannes. Family members frequently accompanied her on these trips but her sadness at the loss of Fitzroy remained with her. She died at Letham Grange in 1932 and was buried alongside her mother and sister at St Vigeans churchyard.

According to the terms of Fitzroy's Trust, Conway inherited Letham Grange and Fern Estate with all the furnishings and Thomas inherited Ardmulchan, its contents and the pedigree stock of horses.

139. Frances Mary Fletcher with her family at Cannes.
Courtesy of Private Collection.

140. Frances Mary Fletcher with her family at Ardmulchan House.
Courtesy of Private Collection.

Frances Mary made small bequests to her sons Conway and Thomas, her daughter, niece and solicitor; but Thomas, who emerged as her favourite, was made sole executor and beneficiary of the residue of her estate.

As a gesture of the high regard in which both adopted sons held Fitzroy, Conway had an intricate and beautiful stained glass window installed at Fern Church to Fitzroy's memory with the added inscription to the bottom right hand corner.

"To the Glory of God and in loving memory of Fitzroy Charles Fletcher of Letham Grange and Fern, who was born 7th November 1858 and died 5th August 1902, this window is erected by Conway Fletcher of Letham Grange and Fern."

It was perhaps even more significant that Conway had this window fitted on the gable end of the Church which overlooks Fitzroy's grave. The non-traditional inclusion of daffodils to the bottom right and left corners of the window was a specific request of Conway's, daffodils being his favourite flower. Conway died in 1957.

141. Panel from Fern Church Window.
K. MacLeman.

142. The stained glass window at Fern Church - dedicated by Conway Fletcher to the memory of Fitzroy Charles Fletcher.
K. MacLeman.

Thomas had inherited much of his mother's nature and particularly her love of horses and the horse-racing world. Affable and friendly, he enjoyed company and was well respected by all. Having married Mary Isabelle Marion Jackson in 1913, Thomas had already been responsible for the management of Ardmulchan for several years and now took over full control of the estate at the age of fifty.

143. Thomas Fletcher of Ardmulchan.
Courtesy of Private Collection.

As a well-known sportsman he participated regularly in the Meath Hunt but it was on the Irish and English race-courses that his horses figured most prominently: the most notable of these were "Galway Gate", a champion sprinter and "O'Malley Mor", one of the best two-year olds of its year. In later years he had victories with the well-known hurdlers "On Straight" and "French Chicken". It is reported that "On Straight" received its name from the standard local response to direction enquiries.

144. Thomas Fletcher at Ardmulchan.
Courtesy of Private Collection.

Thomas was a director of the Proudstown Park racecourse from its inception in 1921, an interest which he maintained to his death, and his strenuous and loyal efforts through good and bad economic times were responsible for the Navan venue becoming the popular and leading place it occupied in the racing life of Ireland.

As a keen agriculturalist and a great judge of cattle, Thomas could not have become owner of Armulchan Estate at a more inopportune time. A dramatic drop in world prices for grain and cattle had wreaked havoc in the economic situation of tenant farmers both in Ireland and Britain and many farmers were forced to dispose of crops and shoot animals which could not be sold. The situation was at its lowest point in 1932 and with the revenue from the estate being likewise depressed, Thomas found himself having to follow the example of other landowners, and so rented out Ardmulchan. One of the more important tenants was Sir Alexander Maguire who leased it from 1936 to 1939.

145. The proud angler with his catch from the Boyne,
a 30lbs. plus salmon.
Thomas Fletcher at Ardmulchan.
Courtesy of Private Collection.

146. Threshing at Ardmulchan.
Courtesy of Private Collection.

147. Harvesting at Ardmulchan.
Courtesy of Private Collection.

With the outbreak of another World War, life for Thomas Fletcher and his family suffered changes no different from other families; but the era of the country estate, loyal servants and sporting life had been destroyed. In the post-war years, the family moved from Ardmulchan House to Dunmoe Cottage which was on the other bank of the Boyne directly opposite Ardmulchan. This may well have served as a constant reminder of a bygone era and it was here that Thomas died in December 1950. Ownership of the Ardmulchan Estate was then transferred from the Fletcher family to Mr and Mrs Riddell Martin in 1956.

Two quotes from the Obituary in the Meath Chronicle of December 1950 indicate clearly how much Thomas had endeared himself to the local community,

"In Dunmoe and Ardmulchan he gave a great deal of employment and as an employer he had few equals and no superiors."

And surely no greater compliment could be paid to one born in Australia and reared in Scotland than,

"Kindly and considerate, he was a very fine type of Irish country gentleman and his passing is widely regretted."

It was therefore immensely appropriate that he was buried in his much-loved County Meath.

148. View of Ardmulchan from Dunmoe.

"And here the true beauties of the Boyne - which simple prose cannot describe".
Sir William Wilde.

POSTSCRIPT.

Cottages, houses, mansions - all are "machines for living in," and like machines they function better when they are in constant use and well maintained. Wealthy landowners provided a great deal of employment in country areas; but education and travel - so well supported by James Fletcher - were in fact contributory factors to the ending of this "grand" lifestyle. "Machines" cannot function without integral parts - in this case, the servants.

Wealth, design and craftsmanship were no guarantee of a perpetuating existence for the great houses. Size and position plays an important part in the struggle for survival, as does the fickleness of modern taste. James Douglas Fletcher had built large and ostentatiously and a house expected to last hundreds of years lasted barely sixty. James Fletcher and Fitzroy had built more moderately and though Letham Grange suffered the deprivation of some empty years, a conversion to an hotel with leisure activities has sustained it. The extensive policies, however, have been given over to private housing - a necessary transformation.

Ardmulchan has survived successfully and remains a private abode. Since 1956, modernising and personal alterations have been made through changes of ownership but it retains its original identity and endures.

Ardmulchan Castle

APPENDIX

This section has been included purely for interest.

The wedding of Constance Maud Fletcher took place in the Inverness Cathedral on the 2nd of November 1876. On the Tuesday evening prior to the marriage, a deputation representing the tenants of Rosehaugh Estate presented Miss Constance Fletcher with a magnificent silver epergne and silver claret jug. The deputation consisted of Mr. Holehouse, Mount Pleasant; Mr. Petrie, Easter Suddie; Mr. Logan, Corrachie; Mr. Singer, Limekilns; Mr Stevenson, Avoch Mills and Mr. Nicol Miller, Avoch. Mr. Robertson, in the absence of Mr. A Ross, architect of Inverness presented a massive marble clock with ornamental vases on behalf of the contractors and tradesmen employed on Rosehaugh Estate. After cake and wine, the wedding presents were inspected and the deputation left.

With one hundred and twenty guests arriving at Inverness Cathedral on the wedding morning, the number of carriages rolling through the streets created considerable excitement. The wedding breakfast was served in the Caledonian Hotel and the French used in the menu was that of the chef's: -

Wedding Breakfast Menu.
Potages (Soup) - Mock Turtle; Brown Windsor.
Entries (First Course) - Mutton cutlets and peas; chicken fricassee with truffles; spiced calf's sweetbread; stewed venison fillets.
Releves Froid (Cold Meats) - Galantine of turkey stuffed with truffles; dressed ham; roast chicken; rolled sirloin; young roast turkey and young partridge; dressed ox-tongue; lobster with salad dressing and oysters on ice; pheasant and game pate; fillet of sole in aspic; London crabs; side of roast lamb; grouse; pheasant; black cock grouse; jellied chicken fillets.
Entremets (Side dishes) - Fruit salad jelly; maraschino custard; stewed apricots; iced Genoa sponge; Charlotte Russe; cabinet pudding; various pastries; Neapolitan and Savoy sponge.
Glaces (Ices) - Vanilla ice cream; lemonade.

A dinner and ball took place at the Rosehaugh home farm steading to which nearly four hundred ladies and gentlemen accepted an invitation. Dinner commenced at five o'clock in the afternoon at which only gentlemen were present, three hundred in number. Ample stabling was available for the horses of the many coaches, and the dinner and later ballroom refreshments were catered for by Mr. Grant of the Munlochy Inn. So many and long were the speeches at dinner that it continued until half past nine when the ballroom was opened. Mr. Logan's string orchestra from Inverness provided the music for dancing which went on till four o'clock in the morning. Supper had been served at two o'clock and refreshments were available throughout the evening.

ACKNOWLEDGEMENTS.

My grateful thanks are due to the many who contributed in almost five years of research. Special thanks are due to the members of the Fletcher Family without whom this book would not have been possible. I would also like to acknowledge the librarians, archivists and others, who made great efforts on my behalf. Over such a long period, I do apologise if I have unintentionally omitted anyone from the list below. Every effort has been made regarding copyright and should any infringement have occurred, I hope to be forgiven.

Special thanks go to: -
Mr. & Mrs. Andrew
Angus Council - Mrs. P. Kennedy, Mr Jepson
Angus Council, Cultural Services
Arbroath Library - Teresa Roby
Arbroath Museum - Fiona Guest, May Gault
Ardmulchan Estates
Ardverikie Estates Ltd.
Brian Austen, Furniture History Society
Tricia Bell
Andy Bennett - Meath County Library
Conor Brennan
R. Dobbie
Dunc & Margery Fraser
Sean Galvin
Douglas Gibson
John Gifford, Buildings of Scotland
Gilbert Library, Dublin - Maire Kennedy
Joelle Gilbert
Duncan Gordon
Helen Gordon
Sandy Gracie RIBA, ARIAS
Haddington Local History Centre - Veronica Wallace
Hilda Hesling

Highland Council Archives - Staff
Highland Council Planning Department
Highland Folk Museum - Rachael Chisholm
Inverness Reference Library - Staff
Anne Jack
D. Jack
Letham Grange Hotel Management
Court of the Lord Lyon
Eileen MacAskill
Patrick MacDonnell, Drogheda Port Company
C. & G. MacKenzie, Melvin House Hotel
Dunc & Margery MacKenzie
Alastair MacLeod - Highland Genealogist
Mather Family - Shandford
Montrose Archives - Fiona Scharlau, Joelle Gilbert
Emer Mooney, Personal Assistant, Slane Castle
Napier University, Edinburgh
National Library of Ireland
National Library of Scotland
National Maritime Museum - Eleanor Heron
National Photographic Archive, Dublin - G. MacLochlainn
National Portrait Gallery of Scotland
Norman Newton - Senior Librarian, Highland Libraries
Aline Oag
Jenny Park, Information Officer, University of Abertay
James Riley
RCAHMS - Veronica Steele, Lesley Ferguson, Staff
Fiona Scharlau
John Shaw of Tordarroch
David Vernon
John Weir DA, RIBA, ARIAS
Maureen Whyte

ILLUSTRATIONS.

Front Cover   Letham Grange circa 1890. Courtesy of Private Collection.   Ardmulchan - K. MacLeman.
Back Cover   Fitzroy C. Fletcher. Courtesy of Private Collection.
Frontispiece The Arms of Fitzroy Fletcher - Dublin.
ii   Fitzroy Charles Fletcher. Courtesy of Private Collection.
iv   The Stephen, Hamilton and Grant Family Tree.
1a.   Map of Australia - pre 1828. Page 2.
1b.   Map of Australia - circa 1855. Page 2.
2.   The Prince Regent. Courtesy of National Maritime Museum. Page 4.
3.   Portrait of Sidney Stephen. Page 6.
4.   Photograph of Sir Alfred Stephen. Page 8.
5.   The Arms of Sir Alfred Stephen. Page 9.
6.   Map of the Melbourne area - circa 1855. Page 13.
7.   Frederica Mary Stephen. Courtesy of John Shaw of Tordarroch. Page 15.
8.   Westertown - Seat of Colonel Hay. Page 17.
9.   The letter of 1854 from W. Pasmore. Page 19.
10.   Portrait of Constance Fletcher by Colin Hunter. Courtesy of John Shaw of Tordarroch. Page 22.
11.   Portrait of James Fletcher by Colin Hunter. Courtesy of Private Collection. Page 23.
12.   Fitzroy Fletcher in the uniform of the Royal Scots Greys. Courtesy of Private Collection. Page 25.
13.   Map showing the sites of the Letham, Peebles and New Grange Estates. Page 28.
14.   Letham Grange - 1827 by Archibald Simpson. Page 29.
15.   Part of the entrance arch and gates of Letham Grange. Page 30.
16.   Fortrose Drill Hall by John Robertson 1881. Page 34.
17.   Advertisement for the hire of the Drill Hall. Page 35.
18.   Fortrose Academy by John Robertson 1890. Courtesy of Highland Council Archives. Page 37.
19.   The Robertson of Inshes Mausoleum. Page 38

20.	Ardverikie House by John Rhind 1871 to 1878. K. MacLeman. Page 41.
21.	The turrets of Ardverikie. K. MacLeman. Page 42.
22.	The ornate ironwork of Ardverikie. K. MacLeman. Page 42.
23.	The walls of Ardverikie Hall. K. MacLeman. Page 43.
24.	One of the wooden panels of Ardverikie Hall. K. Macleman. Page 43.
25.	The hall arch at Ardverikie. K. MacLeman. Page 44.
26.	One of the hall doors at Ardverikie. K. MacLeman. Page 44.
27.	John Rhind - 1836 to 1889. K. MacLeman. Page 46.
28.	Lochardil by John Rhind 1876. K. MacLeman. Page 47.
29.	Inverness High Public School by John Rhind 1878. K. MacLeman. Page 47.
30.	Letham Grange by Archibald Simpson. Page 48.
31.	Letham Grange by John Robertson and John Rhind 1880 to 1885. Page 48.
32.	Drawing of Letham Grange circa 1885. Page 51.
33.	The tower of Letham Grange. K. MacLeman. Page 52.
34.	The entrance of Letham Grange. K. Macleman. Page 54.
35.	The open area opposite the rear door of Letham Grange. Courtesy of Private Collection. Page 55.
36a.	Ground floor plan by Sandy Gracie. Page 56.
36b.	Ground floor plan by Sandy Gracie. Page 57.
37.	The doorway of the Morning Room. K. MacLeman. Page 59.
38.	The Dining Room - circa 1900. Courtesy of Private Collection. Page 61.
39.	The fireplace of the Dining Room. K. MacLeman. Page 62.
40.	The ceiling pendant of the Dining Room. K. MacLeman. Page 63.
41.	Plan of south section - circa 1887. Ritchie and Dick, K. MacLeman. Page 64.

42. Plan of north section - circa 1887. Ritchie and Dick, K. MacLeman. Page 65.
43. The fireplace of the Drawing Room. K. MacLeman. Page 66.
44. The Drawing Room circa 1900. Courtesy of Private Collection. Page 67.
45. The cornice of the Drawing Room. K. Macleman. Page 68
46. The wide doorway of the Drawing Room. K. Macleman. Page 68.
47. The conservatory of 1885. Courtesy of Private Collection. Page 69.
48. Photograph of Letham Grange by Anckorn of Arbroath circa 1900. Courtesy of Private Collection. Page 70.
49. The voice piece in the Billiard Room. K. Macleman. Page 71.
50. The fireplace of the Billiard Room. K. Macleman. Page 72
51. The doorway of the Billiard Room. K. Macleman. Page 72
52. The main stairway. K. Macleman. Page 73.
53. The portrait of James Fletcher in the stairwell. K. Macleman. Page 73.
54. Plan of the south section of the first floor. Ritchie and Dick, K. Macleman. Page 74.
55. Plan of the north section of the first floor. Ritchie and Dick, K. MacLeman. Page 75.
56. The first floor corridor circa 1900. Courtesy of Private Collection. Page 76.
57. Plan of the south section of top floor. Ritchie and Dick, K. MacLeman. Page 78.
58. Plan of the north section of the top floor. Ritchie and Dick, K. Macleman. Page 79.
59. Plan of the basement. Ritchie and Dick, K. MacLeman. Page 81.
60. Letham Grange in the 1990s. K. Macleman. Page 83.

61. Fitzroy Charles Fletcher. Courtesy of Private Collection. Page 84.
62. Miss Ellaline Terriss. Courtesy of Private Collection. Page 86.
63. Frances Mary Grant, later Fletcher. Courtesy of Private Collection. Page 87.
64. Shandford Lodge, Fern. K. Macleman. Page 89.
65. The stone tablet at Shandford Lodge bearing the initials of Fitzroy C. Fletcher. K. Macleman. Page 89.
66. In anticipation of a successful day's shooting. Courtesy of H. Gordon. Page 90.
67. The stone tablet bearing a Latin inscription at Fern Library. K. Macleman. Page 92.
68. Fern Library. K. Macleman. Page 93.
69. Fitzroy Fletcher photographed on a hunter. Courtesy of Private Collection. Page 95.
70. The Arms of Fitzroy Fletcher. Page 96.
71. Jock, the Scottish collie. Courtesy of Private Collection. Page 97.
72. Fitzroy Fletcher with Jock. Courtesy of Private Collection. Page 98.
73. The grave of Fitzroy Fletcher. K. Macleman. Page 100.
74. Fitzroy Fletcher. Courtesy of Private Collection. Page 101.
75. The artificial lake at Letham Grange. K. Macleman. Page 102.
76. The stables at Letham Grange home farm 1896. Courtesy of Private Collection. Page 105.
77. The stables and coach-house at Letham Grange 1896. Courtesy of Private Collection. Page 106.
78. Plans of the hothouses at Letham Grange from the Mackenzie & Moncur catalogue. Crown Copyright: R.C.A.H.M.S. Page 108.
79. The hothouses built by Mackenzie & Moncur. Courtesy of Private Collection. Page 109.
80. The hothouses and walled garden at Letham Grange. Courtesy of Private Collection. Page 109.

81. An abundance of grapes at Letham Grange. Courtesy of Private Collection. Page 110.
82. The heating system in the vinery at Letham Grange. Courtesy of Private Collection. Page 111.
83. The miniature locomotive at Letham Grange. Courtesy of Private Collection. Page 112.
84. Preparations for the Hunt at Ardmulchan. Courtesy of Private Collection. Page 115.
85. A stable in Ireland circa 1900. Courtesy of Private Collection. Page 115.
86. Map of County Meath. Page 116.
87. Map of the River Boyne from Drogheda to Navan. Page 117.
88. The River Boyne at Slane. Courtesy of the National Library of Ireland - Lawrence Collection NS 8713. Page 119.
89. The remains of Dunmoe Castle. K. Macleman. Page 121.
90. The Banks of the Boyne and Dunmoe Ruins. Page 123.
91. Portrait of Sydney Mitchell. Crown Copyright: R.C.A.H.M.S. Page 124.
92. Rothesay Terrace. K. Macleman. Page 127.
93. The porch of 3 Rothesay Terrace. K. Macleman. Page 127.
94. The stairwell at 3 Rothesay Terrace. K. Macleman. Page 128.
95. The griffins and newels of the stairs. K. Macleman. Page 128.
96. The frieze of the Banqueting Room. K. Macleman. Page 129.
97. One of the personalised windows. K. Macleman. Page 130.
98. The overmantel of the Banqueting Room. K. Macleman. Page 130.
99. The fireplace of the Banqueting Room. K. Macleman. Page 131.
100. The fireplace of the Drawing Room. K. Macleman. Page 132.
101. A ceiling panel of the Drawing Room. K. Macleman. Page 133.
102. A side ceiling panel of the Drawing Room. K. Macleman Page 133.
103. The fireplace of the Library. K. Macleman. Page 134.
104. Some brass escutcheons. K. Macleman. Page 135.
105. The minstrels gallery in the Library. K. Macleman. Page 135.

106. The central building of New Craighouse. K. Macleman. Page 137.
107. The hall ceiling at New Craighouse. K. Macleman. Page 137.
108. The west window and ceiling of the hall. K. Macleman. Page 138.
109. Part of the east section of the hall. K. Macleman. Page 138.
110. The Morning Room at the Pleasance circa 1900. Crown Copyright : R.C.A.H.M.S. Page 140.
111. The Hallway at the Pleasance circa 1900. Crown Copyright: R.C.A.H.M.S. Page 140.
112. The Drawing Room at the Pleasance circa 1900. Crown Copyright : R.C.A.H.M.S. Page 141.
113. The Ardmulchan House of the Taafe Family. Courtesy of Private Collection. Page 142.
114. Slane Castle. K. Macleman. Page 143.
115. The letter from Sydney Mitchell to Fitzroy Fletcher 1901. Courtesy of Private Collection. Page 146.
116. The port of Drogheda circa 1900. Courtesy of the National Library of Ireland. The Lawrence Collection IMP 3826. Page 147.
117. Extract from the Arbroath Harbour records. Kind permission of Angus Council Cultural Services. Page 148.
118. The front entrance of Ardmulchan. K. Macleman. Page 150.
119. Photograph of Ardmulchan on completion. Courtesy of Private Collection. Page 151.
120. The north side of Ardmulchan showing the three bays and connecting sections. K. Macleman. Page 152.
121. The southwest pier of the tower which housed the water tanks. K. Macleman. Page 153.
122. The mullioned window. K. Macleman. Page 155.
123. The Dining Room fireplace at Rosehaugh. Thomas Love & Sons, Perth. Page 156.
124. The Dining Room fireplace at Ardmulchan. Courtesy of Private Collection. Page 157.
125. One of the baths at Rosehaugh. D. Macleman. Courtesy of Avoch Heritage Association. Page 158.

126. The power house at Ardmulchan. K. Macleman. Page 160.
127. The gardens of Ardmulchan. K. Macleman. Page 161.
128. Frances Mary Fletcher, her mother and Thomas at the door of Ardmulchan soon after completion. Courtesy of Private Collection. Page 162.
129. Ardmulchan. Courtesy of Private Collection. Page 163.
130. Frances Mary Grant later Fletcher. Courtesy of Private Collection. Page 164.
131. The riding school building at Letham Grange. K. Macleman. Page 167.
132. Mary Grant with her grandson Thomas in the walled garden at Letham Grange. Courtesy of Private Collection. Page 167.
133. The Unionist Garden Party at Letham Grange 1919. Page 168.
134. Conway Fletcher in Ceylon 1911. Courtesy of Private Collection. Page 170.
135. Thomas Fletcher in Egypt 1911. Courtesy of Private Collection. Page 170.
136. Conway and Thomas Fletcher at Dambrilla, Ceylon 1911. Courtesy of Private Collection. Page 171.
137. Conway Fletcher at Hapugah, Ceylon 1911. Courtesy of Private Collection. Page 171.
138. Frances Mary Fletcher at Letham Grange 1920. Courtesy of Private Collection. Page 172.
139. Frances Mary and her family at Cannes. Courtesy of Private Collection. Page 173.
140. Frances Mary and her family at Ardmulchan. Courtesy of Private Collection. Page 173.
141. A panel from Fern Church glass window. K. MacLeman. Page 174.
142. The stained glass window at Fern Church. K. MacLeman. Page 175.
143. Thomas Fletcher of Ardmulchan. Courtesy of Private Collection. Page 176.
144. Thomas Fletcher at the door of Ardmulchan. Courtesy of Private Collection. Page 177.

145. Thomas Fletcher with his catch from the Boyne. Courtesy of Private Collection. Page 178.
146. Threshing at Ardmulchan. Courtesy of Private Collection. Page 179.
147. Harvesting at Ardmulchan. Courtesy of Private Collection. Page 180.
148. View of Ardmulchan from Dunmoe. K. MacLeman. Page 182.
149. Ardmulchan Castle. Page 184.

BIBLIOGRAPHY AND GENERAL READING

THE PIONEER FAMILIES

ANGUS & ROBERTSON - Australian Encyclopaedia.
BURKE - Colonial Gentry
BURKE - Landed Gentry
HISTORICAL RECORDS OF AUSTRALIA
AUSTRALIAN PORTRAIT GALLERY
DICTIONARY OF NEW ZEALAND - Biographies
PIONEER FAMILIES OF AUSTRALIA
WATSON, Don - Caledonia Australis
HEWITSON, Jim - Far Off in Sunlit Places
RUSSELL, Helen - The Past around Us
FAIRBURN - Book of Crests
BURKE - General Armoury
WADE, W. Cecil - Symbolism of Heraldry
PARKER, James - Glossary of Terms in Heraldry
Old Parish Records of Kingussie

FREDERICA MARY STEPHEN

PIONEER FAMILIES OF AUSTRALIA
MILLS, J AND OTHERS - Rosehaugh, A House of its Time
BARNES with ALLEN - Uniforms & History of Scottish Regiments.
ELGIN - Its Situation, Soil and Climate.
WATSON, J&W, Morayshire Described 1868
Census Records in Liverpool
Inverness Courier - Report of November 1876

HISTORY OF LETHAM GRANGE
Newspaper Cuttings - 1897
Arbroath Guide - 1920
Forfarshire Cuttings - 1880
FRENCH, Noel E. - Navan by the Boyne.

ROSS, ROBERTSON & RHIND

Valuation Rolls; Census Returns; Parish Records;
Inverness Old High Church - pamphlet
Inverness Courier & Scottish Highlander - 1889
SLATERS - Trade Directory of Scotland 1860
GIFFORD, John - Buildings of Scotland, Highlands and Islands
GLENDINNING, MACINNES & MACKECHNIE - History of Scottish Architecture.
GRANT, Eliza - Memoirs of a Highland Lady
MACKENZIE, Campbell - Dissertation 1990, MacIntosh Sch. Glas.
ORAM, Richard - Moray & Badenoch Historical Guide
RCAHMS - Listings of Architects and Commissions
Romantic Badenoch - Guide Book
USHER, N - Annals of a Highland Parish

THE MANSION OF LETHAM GRANGE

Forfarshire Cuttings 1880
Journal of Decorative Art V 9/1885 P770
Building News XLIX P470
Plans of R.W. Ritchie & Dick
Plan of Sandy Gracie RIBA, ARIAS
MACKENZIE & MONCUR - Catalogue of 1907
SLATERS - Trade Directory of 1860
WARD, LOCK & CO - The Enquirer's Oracle
CARRUTHERS, Annette - Scottish Home (NMS)
SYMONDS & WHINERAY - Victorian Furniture P41

FITZROY C. FLETCHER

Arbroath Herald and Arbroath Guide newspaper cuttings
BURKE - Landed Gentry of Ireland
PARKER, James - Glossary of Terms used in Heraldry

LETHAM GRANGE ESTATE

Minutes of the Angus Agricultural Association
Arbroath Herald and Arbroath Guide newspaper cuttings

COUNTY MEATH, BOYNE & ARDMULCHAN

FRENCH, Noel E - Navan by the Boyne
ELLISON, Cyril - The waters of the Boyne and Blackwater
BOYLAN, Henry - A Valley of Kings, The Boyne.
WILDE, Sir William - The beauties of the Boyne and Blackwater.
LEWIS, Colin A - Hunting in Ireland
FRENCH, Noel E - The Story of Farming in County Meath
Civil Survey of Ardmulchan Parish - 1654
Ordinance Survey of Ardmulchan Parish - 1836
Meath Chronicle cuttings of Mrs Elizabeth Hickey's account of Ardmulchan.

ARTHUR GEORGE SYDNEY MITCHELL

RCAHMS - records
GLENDINNING, MACINNES & MACKECHNIE - History of Scottish Architecture.
WEIR, John D, DA (Edin.) RIBA, ARIAS - Unpublished Article on Sydney Mitchell and George Wilson.
NAPIER UNIVERSITY - Booklet on Craighouse
McWILLIAM, Colin - Lothian except Edinburgh (Buildings of Scotland series) 1978
Valuation Rolls and Public Records

ARDMULCHAN HOUSE
Records of Arbroath Harbour
Records of Drogheda Port
Personal letter from Sydney Mitchell to Fitzroy Fletcher

BRENNAN, Conor - Yellow Furze Memories
CASEY, C & ROWAN, A - Buildings of Ireland (North Leinster)
BENCE-JONES, Mark - Burke's Guide to Country Houses- Vol.1

FRANCES MARY GRANT, CONWAY & THOMAS

Newspaper cuttings from Arbroath Herald and Meath Chronicle
PIONEER FAMILIES OF AUSTRALIA
WALFORD 1921 EDITION - THE UNITED KINGDOM

INDEX

"Abberton", 11
Abbot William, 27
Abercorn, Duke of, 40
Abercromby Pl. Edin. 20
"Admiral Cockburn", 10
Anderson, George & Co. 50
Anderson, John, 50
Anderson, Sir Rowand, 125,136
Angus Agric. Ass. 103
Angus Show, 103
Arbroath, 27,28,85,103
Arbroath Harbour, 145
Arbroath Infirmary, 85
Arbroath Pipe Band, 169
Arbroath Railway, 49
Arctic Circle, 113
Ardbraccan, 144
Ardmulchan, 27,50,94,99,100, 120-122.
Ardmulchan Castle, 143-163
    Construction, 144-149
    Exterior, 149-153
    Mullioned window, 154,155
    Interior, 154-159
    Grounds, 160,161
Ardmulkin Parish, 121,122
Ard Mullachain, 120
Ardverikie, 40,42,43,45
Arms of Fitzroy Fletcher, 96
Arms of Sir Alfred Stephen, 9
Auckland, NZ. 16
Australia -
    Eldersie, 11
    Ballarat, 13
    Bass Strait, 11
    Bendigo, 13

Bentley Hotel, 14
Bunnyong, 13
Cairnhill, 11
Castlemaine, 13
Eureka Stockade, 13,14
Gisbourne, 11
Hobart, 5,7
Melbourne,6,10,11,13,14,15, 18,21,99,165
New Gisbourne, 11
New South Wales, 5,13,16
Port Macquarie, 16
Port Phillip, 11
St. Kilda, 10
Sydney, 2,5,7,10,11,12,15
Tasmania, 11
Van Diemen's Land, 5,7
Victoria, 2,11,13,14,18
Avoch Free Church, 33
Badenoch, 39, 40
"Badger", 145
Balavil Estate, 12
Balmoral, 40
Banff, 39
Barony of Skreen, 121
"Barraconda", 145
Baxter, Lady, 169
"Beaver", 145
Beaufort Scale, 113
Beaufort Sea, 113
Beaufort, Ad. Sir Francis, 113
Bedford Lemere & Co. 139
Black Isle, 33,36,39,60
Bonnington, 28
Boyne Canal, 118,120,122
Boyne Navigation Co.118,120,122

Boyne River, 113,116,118,120,121, 122,144,149,152,161,181
Braeruthven, 12
Brechin, 32,53,99,103
Brechin Mart, 99
Brennan, Conor, 160,161
British West Indies, 3
Brodie of Brodie, 165
Brodies, Edin. 99
Brothock, 29
Brown, John, 27
Bryce, David, 136
Cairnhill, Scot. 11
Caledonian Canal, 31
Caledonian Kings, 40
Californian Gold Rush, 12,13
Campbell, Margaret, 32
Cannes, 172,173
Carlisle, Thomas, 126
Ceylon, 100,170,171
"Challenge" Landseer, 40
Chambers & Thurlow, 12
Chanonry Point, 31
Civil Survey 1654-Meath, 121
Clouston, Dr. 136
Clouston Chateau, 136
Colliston, 50
Colliston & St. Vig. Ass. 169
Conyngham, Marquis of, 94,143
County Kildare, 116
County Meath, 94,113,120,166,181
Craighouse, Edin. 136-138
Cromarty, 31
Cromdale, 125
Crown Court Church, Strand, 88
Cunard, 21
Dambrilla, Ceylon, 171
Dean Village, 126,132

Deuveaux, Capt. 91
Disruption of Church of Scot. 32
Donaghmore, 121
Dowth, 113
Dowth Hall, 144
Drogheda, 113,116,118,120,122, 145,149
Drummond Pl. Edin. 125,141
Dublin, 114,120,154,166
"Dundalk", 31
Dunmoe Castle, 121,149
Dunmoe Cottage,161, 181
Edin. Medical Sch. 126
Eton, 21,24
Fagan, Mrs. 169
Farquharson, 50
Ferguson, Dr. 91
Fern, 26,88,91,92,99
Fern Church, 92,99
Fern Library, 91,92,93,94
Fern, Shandford Lodge, 88,89
Fern, Stained glass window, 174,175
Fingall, 10th Earl of, 94
Finlay, John Ritchie, 126
Fletcher -
  Alfred Nevett, 21,166
  Constance Maud, 21,24
  Conway, 88,100,165,169,170, 171,172,174
  Edward Stephen, 21
  Fitzroy Charles,
  Agricultural interests, 103,104
  Ardmulchan, 94,143-149,162
  Death, 99,100
  Early life, 20,21,24
  Fern, 88-93
  Hunting, 94

Letham Estate, 104-111
Marriage, 88
Public service, 85
References, 60,63,69,71,82,183
Frances Mary, 14
Ardmulchan, 143,162
Fern Library, 91
France, 172
Garden Party, 169
Life after Fitzroy, 165-172
Life with Fitzroy, 88,99,100
MacGrath, 166
Frederica Mary, 10,15,16,18,20
James,
Marriage, 18
Children, 20,21,24,26
Letham, 27,29,33,36,49,53,60, 77,82
Rosehaugh, 32,33,60
Postscript, 183
James Douglas, 21,24,26,88,97, 104,139,183
Thomas, 88,100,162,165,170, 171,172,174,176 - 181.
Flockhart, William, 144,160
Fohbar, 27
Forfarshire, 27
Fortrose, 33
Fortrose Academy, 36
Fortrose, Drill hall, 36
Fortrose, Free Church manse, 36
Fortrose, Priory, 36
"French Chicken", 176
"Galway Gate", 176
George St. Edin. 125,136
Gracie, Sandy, 56,57
Gradwell, Robert, 91,94,144

Grant -
Frances Mary, (see Fletcher)
Isobel Eliz. (see Hamilton)
James MacPherson, 12,13,14, 88,165
Lewis, 12
Mary, 88,166
Grant, Edith, Woodside, 169
Gullane, 139
Guthrie, Alfred, 50
Haddo, Lord, 139
Hamilton -
Georgina Jane, 11,21,166
Isabel Eliz, (was Grant), 166
Col. John Ferrier, 11
John Ferrier, 11,166
Thomas Ferrier, 11,21
Hamilton, Mary Matthew, (see Stephen.)
Hapugah, Ceylon, 171
Harrow & Sinclair, 50
Hay, Col. Alex. 16
Hay, Alex. MacLeod, 16
Hay, Alex. 28
Hay, David, 16
Hay, John(Squire), 29,49
Hay, Mary MacLeod, 16,20
Hay, William, 50
Hebrides, 1
Heem, Hugo, 27
Hicks, Sir Seymour, 85
Highlands, 31,125
Holmes, Miss, 169
Hope, Capt. Montagu, 21
Hope, Violet Mary, 165
Horse-racing, 176,177
Houston, Marg. Hay, 125,141
Howard & Sons, 50
Hunting, 94,114

Inverness -
  Bishop's Palace, 39
  Castle St. 39
  Castlehill of Inshes, 32
  Cathedral, 39
  Courier, 1
  Hawthornedean, 38
  Old High Church, 38,45
  Portland Place, 45
  Union St. 33
Irish Grand National, 114
Isle of Skye, 1,39
Jack, James, 18
Jackson, Mary Isabel Marion, 176
Jersey, 10
Jock, collie, 97,98
Jock's Wood, 97
"Kangaroo", 31
Kells, Book of, 113
Kent, A.T. 91
Kew Gardens, 99
Kincraig, 39
Kingussie, 12
Knowth, 113
Landseer, Sir Edwin, 40
Larbert, 125
Latin translation, 93
Leeward Islands, 3
Letham Estate, 27,28,104,105,107,120
Letham Grange - 26,27,28,32, 33,36,46,49,94,144,145,149,183
  Basement, 80,81
  Billiard Rm. 69,71,72
  Conservatory, 69,99
  Dining Rm. 60,61,62,63
  Drawing Rm. 63,66,67,68
  First Floor, 76,77
  Library, 69,77
  Morning Rm.58,59,60
  Riding School, 165
  Rosehaugh Rm. 60
  Top Floor, 77
  Tower, 36,52,76,152
Lochaber, 39
MacBain, Isobel, 12
MacDonald, F.F. Cliff House, 169
MacGrath, Redmond Walter, 166,169
MacGrath, Wm of Toonagh, 166
MacIntosh Family, 32
Mackenzie & Moncur, 107
MacPherson, James, 40
Maguire, Sir Alex. 177
Mail coach, 31
Maitland, Sir J Ramsay, 139
Maori, 12,16
Marlborough, Duke of, 28
Matheson, Sir Alex of Ardross, 32
Mayo, Earl of, 121
McWilliam, Colin, 141
Mealchu's Height, 120
Meath Chronicle, 181
Meath Hunt, 94, 114,144,176
Miln, John Hay, 29
Milne, Isabella, 39
Mitchell, A.G.Sydney, 96,125 - 141,144,145,149,152,154,158,161
Mitchell, George, 125
Mitchell, Sir Arthur, 125,141
Moir, Miss, St Andrews, 169
"Monarch of the Glen", 40
Montagu, Mr. Justice, 5
Montrose, 28
Moy Hall, 45
Muir of Ord, Station Hotel, 36
Musgrave & Co.Ltd. 104,105,107
Navan, 94,113,116,118,120,122,

145
Napier Uni. 136
Nevett, W. 91
New Grange Estate, 28,29
New Grange, Meath, 113
New Zealand, 7,12
Nicoll of Hilton, Mr. 91,92
"O'Malley Mor", 176
Ogle, Billy, 161
"On Straight", 176
Ord. Survey 1836-Meath, 121
Otago, NZ. 6
Pasmore, Mary Ann, 3
Pasmore, Sibylla, 19
Pasmore, Wm. 18,20
Peebles Estate, 28
Perth, 46
Peru, 18
Pleasance, Gullane, 139,141
Plunkett, Henrietta Maria, 94
Pluscarden, Elgin, 16
"Porpoise", 145
"Pride of the Highlands", 104
Prince Albert, 40
"Prince Regent", 4
Privy Council, 5,7
Prospect of Sutherland, 36
Proudstown Park, 177
Queen Anne, 28
Queen Victoria, 40,91
"Rachel", 145
Raigmore House, 32
Ramsden, Sir John Wm. 40,45
Redcastle, Black Isle, 45
Reid, Alex. & Wm. Elgin, 33
Rhind, George, 39
Rhind, John, 33,36,39,40,45,46,53,82
Rhind, Wm. 39,46

Riddell Martin, Mr & Mrs. 181
Riga, Latvia, 145
Ritchie & Dick, 53,54,56,57,64,65,
74,75,78,79,81,82
Robertson of Inshes, 38
Robertson, Alex. 32
Robertson, John, 32,33,46,49,50,53,55
Rome, George & Co. 50,154,159
Rosebery, Earl of, 139
Rosehaugh, 21,24,26,27,29,32,33,
88,104,139,144,154,156,158,159
165,183
Rosehaugh Tea Co. 100
Rosemarkie, Kincurdie, 36
Ross, Alex. 32,33,46,58,82
Ross, James, 32
Rothesay Terr. Edin. 126 ñ134,154
Royal Scots Greys, 24,94
Ruthven Barracks, 12
"Sanctuary", 40
Scots Fusiliers, 28
Scott, Misses, 169
Scottish Educ. Act 1875, 31,91
Shaw, Capt. 169
Shorthorn cattle, 103,104
Simpson, Archibald, 29,32,49
Slane, 118
Slane Castle, 94,143,144
Slane Castle Lock, 122
Society of Antiquaries, 125,139
"Sovereign", 31
St. Andrews Uni. 169
St Kitts, 3,7
St Vigeans, 14,27,28,172
St Fechin, 27
St George's Church, 18
St. Patrick, 113
Stanley, 21

Steers, Thomas, 118
Stephen -
  Claudia, 165
  Eliz. Mary Milner,7,11
  Fitzroy, 10,20,24
  Frances Sidney, 7,14,88,165
  Frederica Mary, 10,15,16,18,
  (later Fletcher)
  James, 3
  James Fitzjames, 3
  John(sen.), 3,5
  John(jun.), 10,11,15,18
  Lilian Maud Augusta, 24
  Mary Matthew, 10,15,20,24
  Sidney, 5,6,10,11,14,88,165
  Sir Alfred, 5,7,8,9,10
Stephen, Robert, 28
Stirling, James, 91,99,111,145
Stirling, James(jun), 111
Taafe Family, 143,144,161
Taafe, Robert, 122
Taafe's Lock, 122
Tara, 113
Taylor, Baillie, 103
Terriss, Ellaline, 85,86
Thackery, Wm. Makepeace, 126
Thompson, Lieu. Col. 20
Thomson, Alex.(Greek), 39
Tomnahurich Cemetery, 46
Trim, 118,120
Tulloch, John, 50
Tweeddale, 21,139
Vandeleur, 21
Wallace & Connell, 50
"Walrus", 145
Well Court, 126
Westerton, 16
Westmeath, 27

"Westmoreland", 10
Westport, Scot. 11
Whyte, James, 50
Wilde, Oscar, 116
Wilde, Sir William, 116
Wills Family, 16
Wilmer, Col. John Randal, 169
Wilmer, Ruby Gordon, 169,171
Wilson, George, 136,144
Wood, Sir James, 28
Woolton Hill House, 18,20,21,26, 94
Wyndham, 21
Wyndham Act 1903, 122
Yellow Furze Memories, 160
Young Architects' Ass. 39
Young St. Edin. 136